Process Metaphysics

SUNY Series in Philosophy

George R. Lucas, Jr., Editor

Process Metaphysics

An Introduction to Process Philosophy

Nicholas Rescher

State University of New York Press

Published by
State University of New York Press

© 1996   State University of New York

Printed in the United States of America

For information, address State University of New York Press,
State University Plaza, Albany, N.Y. 12246

Production by M. R. Mulholland
Marketing by Nancy Farrell

Library of Congress Cataloging-in-Publication Data

Rescher, Nicholas.
    Process metaphysics : an introduction to process philosophy /
Nicholas Rescher.
        p.   cm. — (SUNY series in philosophy)
    Includes bibliographical references and index.
    ISBN 0-7914-2817-6. — ISBN 0-7914-2818-4 (pbk.)
    1. Process philosophy.   I. Title.   II. Series.
BD372.R47   1996
146'.7—dc20   95-8784
                                                             CIP

10 9 8 7 6 5 4 3 2

MUST

IAHY2371

Contents

Preface

The book was written in Pittsburgh during the 1992–1994 academic biennium. It grew out of further reflection on a paper, "The Prospect of Process Philosophy," which I contributed to a conference called Frontiers of American Philosophy, at Texas A&M University in the spring of 1988. The project reflects a longstanding interest in process philosophy, dating back to my first reading of Whitehead's *Process and Reality* in W. T. Stace's seminar at Princeton in 1949 and initially manifesting itself in print over thirty years ago in a paper on "The Revolt against Process" in *The Journal of Philosophy* (vol. 59 [1962], 410–17). I hope the book will induce at least some of its readers among the not already converted to share my sympathetic appreciation of this provocative and fertile philosophical approach.

I am very grateful to Richard Gale and to George R. Lucas, Jr., who have given me some constructive criticisms on draft versions of the book.

Introduction

Process philosophy has in recent years become one of the particularly active and flourishing sectors of American philosophy. Though its antecedents reach back deep into classical antiquity, this doctrine as such is a creation of the twentieth century—in fact, one of its most influential and interesting contributions. As yet, however, no compact introduction to this philosophical approach exists—no conveniently synoptic, compact, and accessible exposition for the use of readers who would like to inform themselves regarding what process philosophy is all about. The aim of the present book is to remedy this lack. It offers a brief but nevertheless comprehensive account of the process approach in metaphysics as a systemic doctrine reaching from Heraclitus to Whitehead and beyond.

One of the characteristic tasks of metaphysics is to articulate the set of concepts and ideational perspectives able to provide a thought-framework for understanding the world about us and our place within it. Such a metaphysical framework need not, of course, be designed to *compete* with the resources afforded us by everyday knowledge and scientific understanding, but can—indeed, should—absorb and supplement them within one comprehensive and harmonious overarching perspective.

Process metaphysics affords one of the most promising and convenient avenues toward realizing this objective. As a venture in what is generally called "speculative metaphysics," process philosophy regards the domain of human knowledge as an organically integrated self-sustaining whole. It does not seek to domineer over—let alone to displace!—our manifold of scientific knowledge, but rather strives to accommodate it. From its angle, the key task of philosophical inquiry is to develop a set of concepts and principles that makes it possible to devise a synoptic and unified yet detailed and substantively adequate descriptive and explanatory account that at once integrates and illuminates our cognitive attainments in science.

Process philosophy here meets with substantial success. Perhaps more effectively than any rival theory, the manifold of ideas revolving around process and activity provides the philosophical resources that enable us to characterize and render intelligible the world's developments as best we can discern them. And here, as elsewhere, our metaphysical conceptions are best validated not just in terms of consonance with our beliefs and convictions but by teleological (functional, purposive) considerations—that is, by showing that the problems we face in trying to understand our situation in the world about us are most efficiently and effectively handled by their means. (Of course, if it could be shown that these conceptions are inevitably required—that adequate understanding is unattainable save by their means—then so much the better. But this is rather too much to ask for.)

Process metaphysics as a general line of approach holds that physical existence is at bottom processual; that processes rather than things best represent the phenomena that we encounter in the natural world about us. The doctrine takes a position within the spectrum of competing following contentions:

1. Process has *primacy* over things. Substance is subordinate to process: Things are simply constellations of processes.
2. Process has *priority* over substance. Things are always subordinate to processes because processes inwardly engender, determine, and characterize the things there are. But processes as such transcend the realm of things since there are also substance-detached processes.
3. Substance has *priority* over process. The only sort of processes there are are those involved in the doings and comportments of things.
4. Substance has *primacy* over process. Indeed, substance is all there is; all processes and changes are simply a matter of how things appear to certain (mind-equipped) substances.

The first two of these competing contentions represent process philosophy respectively in its stronger (Heraclitean) and weaker (Empedoclean) versions. By contrast, the substance approach which process philosophy rejects is represented by the last two contentions. This approach also has a weaker (Democratean) and a stronger (Parmenidean) version. Taken as a whole, the survey indicates the range of positions that lie at the heart of controversy between process and substance philosophy with process metaphysics committed to 1 – or – 2 and substance metaphysics to 2 – or – 3. As this indicates, the divergency at issue here reflects the sort of normative conflict regarding emphasis and fundamentally that is often characteristic of metaphysical disputes.

Like any philosophical movement of larger scale, process philosophy has internal variations. The main difference at issue here has roots in the issue of what type of process is taken as paramount and paradigmatic. Some important contributors, and especially A. N. Whitehead, see physical processes as central and other sorts of processes as modeled on or superengrafted upon them—the conception of an all-integrating physical field being pivotal even for Whitehead's organic/biological reflections. Others (especially Henri Bergson) saw biological processes as fundamental and conceived of the world in essentially organismic terms. Still others (especially William James) based their ideas of process on a psychological model and saw human thought as idealistically paradigmatic. And, consonant with the perspectives as issue here, some (e.g., Whitehead) articulated their process philosophy in essentially scientific terms, while others (especially Bergson) relied more on intuition and, indeed, an almost mystical sort of sympathetic apprehension. All the same, these are differences in style and emphasis that nevertheless leave the teachings of the several processists in the position of variations on a common theme.

Process philosophy represents an attempt to come to intellectual terms with the world's empirical realities by deriving a framework of conceptions and ideas to integrate the products of modern inquiry into a coherent framework of thought linked to a metaphysical tradition reaching from

Heraclitus, Plato, and Aristotle, in antiquity, to Leibniz, at the dawn of the modern age. But while process philosophy (like all else) has a past, it is not of the past and does not belong to it. The central connections of process thinking have a power and generality that qualify it as a position whose insights show ample promise of increasing philosophical utility.

The great promise of a philosophy of process lies in its capacity to fuse into one unifying conception such contrasting polarities as unity and plurality, stability and change, specificity and generality, uniqueness and type. As John Dewey (who, for much of his long career, was a dedicated process philosopher) wrote to William James in 1903:

> It may be the continued working of the Hegelian bacillus of reconciliation in me, that makes me feel as if the conception of process gives a basis for uniting the truths of pluralism and monism, and also of necessity and spontaneity. . . . I cannot help feeling that an adequate analysis of activity would exhibit the world of fact, and the world of ideas as two corresponding objective statements [Dewey means *expressions*] of the active process itself,— correspondent because each has a work to do in the doing of which it needs to be helped by the other.[1]

Any account of a philosophical position as such is bound to have an eclectic aspect in choosing its points of elaboration and emphasis. Some parts of the overall complex suffer comparative deemphasis or neglect and others are highlighted. And this is true of the present discussion as well. It seeks to present an overall and, as it were, "generic" view of process metaphysics and to convey an indication of the spirit of the enterprise. Accordingly it does not—cannot—present (or even everywhere agree with) the overall position of any one particular process philosopher.[2] Rather, it does what it must do, given its aim, by synthesizing a variety of different and sometimes divergent-seeming doctrinal positions into a unified construct that harmonizes with the views that are typical of or predominant in this philosophical tradition.

The English language is a less-than-perfect instrument for discussions of process philosophy if only because of the accordionlike flexibility that ordinary usage gives to the term "thing." The word is simply too ubiquitous and versatile to be dispensed with even the setting of a process-oriented position with its emphasis on the thing/process contrast, particularly so since the word admits a variety of insubstantial applications where *things* in any literal sense of substantial particulars are not necessarily at issue. The item at issue in a "something" locution—for example, "There is something strange going on here"—will often not be a *thing* at all, nor need what is at issue when we say "for another thing" be a *thing* in any literal sense. The reader will, it is hoped, be sufficiently generous to recognize that the use of such "thing" locutions, even in relation to processes, commits no inconsistency and involves no concession to substantialism.

Moreover, we clearly need a word for existents that is not prejudicial as between substances (things) and occurrences (processes, events). Perhaps *phenomena* would serve here insofar as the items at issue are explicitly seen as objects of experience. But if we want to prescind from this, we have to settle for some nondescript term such as *existents* or *reals*—or, if we also wish to abstract even from actual existence, then to speak simply of *items*.

Moreover, English provides only rather insufficient lexical resources for dealing with process issues, and it is convenient to coin a few expressions in an endeavor to make amends.[3] Accordingly, we will adopt the neologism *processual* (or, for occasional variation, *processive*) to stand in for such awkward adjectival hyphenations as "process-geared" and "process-oriented." And it will be convenient to designate the adherents of process and substance philosophy as *processists* and *substantialists*, respectively. By present-day standards of terminological resourcefulness in philosophy, these coinages deserve to be regarded as relatively innocuous.

1

Historical Background

SYNOPSIS

(1) Process philosophy represents an important sector of philosophical tradition. (2) It has a long and distinguished history, going back to the pre-Socratic philosopher Heraclitus, (3) and its development owes much to Plato and Aristotle. Other important processists include: (4) Leibniz, (5) Hegel, (6) C. S. Peirce, (7) William James, (8) Henri Bergson, (9) John Dewey, (10) A. N. Whitehead (11) and W. H. Sheldon. (12) In recent years, process philosophy has been one of the most prominent and active sectors of American philosophy.

1. PROSPECT

The philosophy of process is a venture in metaphysics, the general theory of reality. Its concern is with what exists in the world and with the terms of reference by which this reality is to be understood and explained. The guiding idea of this approach is that natural existence consists in and is best understood in terms of *processes* rather than *things*—of modes of change rather than fixed stabilities. For processists, change of every sort—physical, organic, psychological—is the pervasive and predominant feature of the real.

Process philosophy diametrically opposes the view—as old as Parmenides and Zeno and the Atomists of Pre-Socratic Greece—that denies processes or downgrades them in the order of being or of understanding by subordinating them to substantial things. By contrast, process philosophy pivots on the thesis that the processual nature of existence is a fundamental fact with which any adequate metaphysic must come to terms. The task of metaphysics is, after all, to provide a cogent and plausible account of the nature of reality at the broadest, most synoptic, and most comprehensive level. It seeks to help us understand the nature of things—to characterize and explain the realities we encounter in the world about us and to render intelligible the world as our experience presents it to us. And it is to this mission of enabling us to characterize, describe, clarify, and explain the most general features of the real that process philosophy addresses itself in its own characteristic way.

In recent years, "process philosophy" has virtually become a code word for the doctrines of Alfred North Whitehead and his followers. But, of course, this cannot really be what process philosophy actually is. If there indeed is a "philosophy" of process, it must pivot not on a thinker but on a theory. What is at issue must, in the end, be a philosophical position that has a larger life of its own, apart from any particular exposition or expositor.[1]

What is characteristically definitive of *process* philosophizing as a distinctive sector of philosophical tradition is not simply the commonplace recognition of natural process as the active initiator of what exists in nature but an insistence on seeing process as constituting an essential aspect of everything that exists—a commitment to the fundamentally processual nature of the real. For the process philosopher is, effectively by definition, one who holds that what exists in nature is not just originated and sustained by processes but is in fact ongoingly and inexorably *characterized* by them. On such a view, process is both pervasive in nature and fundamental for its understanding.

To be sure, process philosophy as such is something rather schematic. There are distinct approaches to implementing its pivotal idea of the pervasiveness and fundamentality of process, ranging from a materialism of physical processes (as with Boscovitch) to a speculative idealism of psychic processes (as in some versions of Indian philosophy). The ways of being a process philosopher vary drastically according to the nature of one's ideas regarding what process is all about. We are dealing with a doctrinal tendency and not a particular position.

In historical perspective, process philosophy has run a somewhat meandering course that traces back more to the origins of philosophy in the days of pre-Socratic philosophy. The following discussion presents a rapid Cook's Tour of the highlights of this historical development.

2. HERACLITUS (6TH CENTURY B.C.)

Like so much else in the field, process philosophy began with the ancient Greeks. The Greek theoretician Heraclitus of Ephesus (b. ca. 540 B.C.)—known even in antiquity as "the obscure"—is universally recognized as the founder of the process approach. His book *On Nature* depicted the world as a manifold of opposed forces joined in mutual rivalry, interlocked in constant strife and conflict. Fire is the most changeable and ephemeral of these elemental forces, is bottom of all: "This world-order . . . is . . . an everliving fire, kindling in measures and going out in measures."[2] The fundamental "stuff" of the world is not a material substance of some sort but a natural process, namely, "fire," and all things are products of its workings (*puros tropai*). The variation of different states and conditions of fire—that most process manifesting of the four traditional Greek elements—engenders all natural change, for fire is the destroyer and transformer of things, and "All things happen by strife and necessity" (frag. 211). And this changeability so pervades the world that "one cannot step twice into the same river" (frag. 215).

Heraclitus may accordingly be seen as the founding father of process philosophy (at any rate in the intellectual tradition of the West). And the static system of Parmenides affords its sharpest contrast amid the most radical opposition. However, the paradigm substance philosophy of classical antiquity was the atomism of Leucippus and Democritus and Epicurus which pictured all of nature as composed of unchanging and inert material atoms whose only commerce with process was an alteration of their positioning in space and time. Here the *properties* of substances are never touched by change, which effects only their *relations*.

For Heraclitus, reality is at bottom not a constellation of *things* at all but one of *processes*. As Heraclitus saw it, we must avoid at all costs the fallacy of substantializing nature into perduring things (substances) because they are not stable things but fundamental forces and the varied and fluctuating activities which they produce that make up this world of ours. Process is fundamental: The river is not an *object* but an ever-changing flow; the sun is not a *thing*, but a flaming fire. Everything in nature is a matter of process, of activity, of change. Heraclitus taught that *panta rhei* ("everything flows"), and this principle exerted a profound influence on classical antiquity. Even Plato, who did not much like the principle ("like leaky pots" he added at *Cratylus* 440 C), came to locate his exception to it—the enduring and changeless "ideas"—in a realm wholly removed from the domain of material reality.

3. PLATO AND ARISTOTLE

His endorsement of many Heraclitean teachings makes Plato into a process philosopher of sorts.[3] In various dialogues (especially the *Theaetetus* and the *Timaeus*), he adopted the idea that the perceptible world is thoroughly Heraclitean and processual, unable to provide the stable, orderly foothold required for rational apprehension, description, and explanation. If we are to achieve theoretically adequate knowledge at all, then there must be nonperceptible, unchanging, matter-detached forms ("ideas") for us to get a rational grip on. Accordingly, Plato reasoned as follows:

- The sensory world of our ordinary life experience is through-and-through processual.[4]
- Reason demands stability: Whatever it grasps must be constant, unchanging, timelessly true.

Therefore, if reason is to accomplish its work, there must be another realm, separate from the world of sense, an ideal realm where the demands of reason can be accommodated.

Although Aristotle placed substance at the center of his metaphysics, he, too, had vestigial processist commitments. In a way, he, too, inherited Heraclitean doctrines, seeing that the Aristotelian cosmos manifested stability only at its outer limits with the fixed stars and that all else is pervaded by change. For Aristotle, however, this change itself conforms to inherently natural—and specifically *biological*—patterns, so that the Plato's transcendent "forms" are no longer required.

While Aristotle's metaphysics of substances and natural kinds was an emphatic substantialism, Aristotle's metaphysics nevertheless also deployed a considerable array of processist elements. For, so Aristotle insisted, the "being" of a natural substance is always in transition, involved in the dynamism of change. *Dunamis* (potency), *energeia* (activity), *kinesis* (motion), and *metabolē* (change) are fundamental categories of Aristotelian metaphysics, and he conceives of his particulars developmentally—an acorn is less a stable thing than a stage of an evolving organism moving continually if all goes well, along its predestined journey toward its eventual condition as an oak tree. The programmed directedness of Aristotelian processual particulars that enmesh them in a developmental tendency toward a *telos* (end-state)—and even beyond to decay and death—is a characteristic feature of Aristotelian metaphysics. The natural world, as Aristotle sees it, exhibits a collective dynamism that effects the transit from mere possibilities for a sector of nature to the realization of its full potential, its perfection (*entelecheia*). The Aristotelian view of things is pervasively processual.

Aristotle's position was accordingly something of a halfway house, seeing that his ontology was less one of substances pure and simple than one of substances-in-process. Against Zeno and the Parmenidean tradition (so prominent in Plato), which maintained the ultimate irreality of change, Aristotle upheld the significance of process. The doctrine of causes, the role of activity and passivity among the categories, and the emphasis on change in the theory of physics—all mark Aristotle as one of the key figures in the history of process philosophizing. And, indeed, many of the most pivotal and useful concepts of process thought were introduced into the orbit of philosophical discussion by Aristotle. In fact, the conception of process plays so significant a role in his philosophy that Aristotle, too, deserves a place in this tradition.[5]

With process philosophy, then, as with so much else in the domain of philosophy, the speculations of the thinkers of ancient Greece prepared the way.

4. GOTTFRIED WILHELM LEIBNIZ (1646–1717)

The principal standard bearer of process theory in modern philosophy was Leibniz, who maintained that all of the "things" that figure in our experience, organisms alone excepted, are mere phenomena and not really unified substances at all. The world, in fact, consists of clusters of minute, virtually puncti-form processes he called *monads* (units), which are "centers of force"—in fact, bundles of activity. These monads aggregate together to make up and constitute the world's things as we experience them. But each individual monad is a unit unto itself—an integrated whole of programmed change that denominates it as a single, unified, long-term process.

Although Leibniz is often miscast as a "pluralist"—the exponent of an ontology of many substances—the fact remains that he contemplated only one *type* of "substance" in nature, the *monads*, which actually are nothing but pure processes. Each of these monads is endowed with an inner drive, an "appetition " which ongoingly destabilizes it and provides for a processual course of never-ending change. The whole world is one vast systemic complex of such active processual units. They are programmed agents—"incorporeal automata"— developing in coordinated unison as individual centers of activity operating at different levels of sophistication within an all-comprising unified cosmic whole. Even as a differential equation generates a curve that flows over a mathematical surface, so the internally programmed dynamism of a monad leads it to unfold naturally over the course of time, tracing out its life history from beginning to end. Leibniz accordingly viewed the world as is an infinite collection of agents (monads) linked to one another in an all-pervasive harmony, with each agent, like a member of an orchestra, playing its part in engendering nature's performance as a whole. On this basis, Leibniz developed a complex theory of nature as an integrated assemblage of harmoniously coordinated eventuations so that processes, rather than substantial objects, furnish the basic materials of his ontology.[6]

5. GEORG WILHELM FRIEDRICH HEGEL (1770–1831)

Hegel is prominent among process thinkers because historical development—be it of nature or of thought—lies at the very center of his philosophizing. For Hegel, whatever exists in the world of reality or of ideas is never a stable object but a processual item that is in transit and cannot be properly understood through its stable properties or as a successism of stable states, a matter of now this, now that. It is a process, an item constantly reshaped in an ongoing development proceeding through the operation of a dialectic that continually blends conflicting opposites into a unitary but inherently unstable fusion. Historical change is omnipresent. For Hegel, the real in all its dimensions can be understood and accounted for only in processual terms.[7]

The idea of Concept (*Begriff*) is central in Hegel's thought, but Hegel's concepts or universals are no mere abstractions existing in a static Platonic world-disoriented realm of immaterial pure forms. They are inherently active, and strive for a concrete realization in singularity (*Einzelheit*) so as to exist as particulars in and for thought. They must thus achieve embodiment in the natural world, a standpoint reflected in the notorious theory of self-externalization (*Entäusserung*) of the Absolute Idea of world-history writ large through a dynamic of dialectical development that is the principal conception of Hegel's *Logic*. For Plato, the material realm somehow participates in those static Ideas about which we can learn by an epistemic dialectic; for Hegel, the material world is itself somehow the product of an ontological dialectic driven by an inner dynamic of ideas. What is now pivotal is not idealized order but process, or, rather, that (somewhat mysterious) manifold of processes through which idealized order achieves concretization in nature.

6. CHARLES SANDERS PEIRCE (1839–1914)

Much of traditional philosophy since the ancient Stoics has emphasized the stabilities and fixities characteristic of the world's structure of lawful order. Like Hegel, Peirce rejected this view root and branch. For him, the universe—its lawful order included—is in a state of constant change and development. Not a stability of kinds but a through-and-through process of cosmic evolution characterizes the reality we confront throughout our efforts to understand the world.

The leading metaphysical ideas of Peirce's philosophy of nature (chance [tychism], spontaneity, synechism) are all fundamentally processual, and the whole of his metaphysical position is dynamical and geared to development, evolution, and teleology.[8] The root conception of Peirce's pragmatism—that of a cognitive resource's "proving its utility" in practice—endows his theory of truth and reality with the processual/dynamical aspect that is characteristic of process thought. Even universals are, for Peirce, to be construed in dynamical terms.[9] Like many thinkers of his era, Peirce was deeply impressed by the development of evolutionary theory and saw this selective dynamism at work everywhere—not only in the biological realm but also in the physical cosmos, in its lawful order, and in the development of our knowledge of it. For Peirce, the key to understanding anything that is central in philosophy—nature, value, truth—is provided by the idea of development under the aegis of evolutionary processes.[10]

7. WILLIAM JAMES (1842–1910)

Peirce's congeners in the tradition of American pragmatism continued his juxtaposition of pragmatism and processism. Both William James and John Dewey, for example, developed versions of pragmatism in which the basic ideas of philosophy of process were in one way or another prominent.

For William James, time and the processes that unfold under its aegis are the central issues of metaphysical concern. The human psyche is an organized complex of process, and our affective and cognitive human experience typifies the processual nature of things. Reality, as we humans do and must come to experiential terms with it, is nothing but a structured manifold of processes.[11] James saw the world as a sea of flux comprising a manifold of changes that are not a clear-cut replacement of one hard-edged state by another but a melting and fusing of boundaryless processes that lead into one another. The blooming buzzing confusion of physical process and the ordinary stream of consciousness that provides for structural awareness provide, as James sees it, the key to philosophical understanding of the world's course of things.

James emphasized the ontological centrality of process in terms of "the causal dynamic relatedness of activity and history."[12] He saw nature as engaged in constant—and constantly ineffectual—striving to bring order into chaos and to enforce coherent unity upon an recalcitrant and, indeed, ineliminable diversity and plurality. Such a manifold of activity is a law unto itself—even the classic logical laws of excluded middle and noncontradiction do not bind it, seeing that concrete activity everywhere manifests the potential for breaking out into the most contradictory characterizations.[13] In expressing his agreement with Peirce, James remarked that to "an observer standing outside of its generating causes, novelty can appear only as so much 'chance', while to one who stands inside it is the expression of 'free creative activity'. . . . The common objection to admitting novelties is that by jumping abruptly, *ex nihilo*, they shatter the world's rational continuity."[14] But, he continues, novelty "doesn't arrive by jumps and jolts, it leaks in insensibly, for adjacents in experience are always interfused, the smallest real datum being both a coming and a going."[15] The expression "block universe" served James as a term of derogation, because he scorned and abhorred the idea of a closed world that has no place for novelty and adventure.

Like his spiritual kinsman, Henri Bergson, James believed that arguments along the lines of Zeno's classical paradoxes demonstrated the incapacity of stable concepts to characterize the fluidities of an ever-changing reality. But whereas Bergson looked for escape from conceptual rigidities to the biological sphere, James saw them in the psychological sphere. For him, it is the nature of human experience which, above all, prevents the imposition of conceptual fixities from giving an adequate account of reality. Accordingly, James strongly emphasized the processual nature of experience:

> Now the immensely greater part of all our knowing . . . never is completed or nailed down . . . [but] each experience runs by cognitive transition into the next one. . . . We live, as it were, upon the front edge of an advancing wave-crest, and our sense of a determinate direction in falling forward is all we cover of the future of our path.[16]

James's worldview of flux, spontaneity, and creative novelty projects a philosophy of substantiality without substance. For James, the ongoing innovations launched by intelligent life characterize the tendency of an ongoingly processual reality to break the rules that have grown too restrictively narrow in an endeavor to forge a new and more effective adjustment to an ever-changing scheme of things. Intelligent action is self-development. "The problem for the [intelligent] man is less what he shall now choose to do than what being he shall now resolve to become."[17] James emphasized that one characteristic mode in which we humans participate in nature's processes is through *choice*, and in choosing—in free action—we both make ourselves and change the world into something that would otherwise be different. Even truth and knowledge come within the realm of the Jamesean dynamism: They are not things we *find* but things we *make*.[18]

8. HENRI BERGSON (1859–1941)

Henri Bergson also regarded process and temporality as pivotal features of the word and, in particular, as central to our human scheme of things where life and consciousness manifest change everywhere. For him, time both affords the matrix for experience and provides the stage setting for reality in nature. But while time is fundamental, it is also elusive, seeing that we experience events in time but not the passage of time as such. We see material things but miss the energy that creates them and makes them go. And human conceptual thought is not adequate for the apprehension of time: All of our "exact" science is merely an approximation that apprehends the statics of reality better than its dynamics, proceeding through time—disjointed mathematical formalisms that are, in themselves, lifeless. Conceptualizing thought is inadequate to the vibrancy of human experience. Reality consists of process but thought deals in stable "things." And herein lies the problem. For

> through all our natural [cognitive] abilities of perceiving and conceiving . . . we believe that immobility is as real as movement . . . [but] we can find a solution to philosophical problems only if we succeed, by a reversal of our mental habits, to see in mobility the only reality that is actual. Immobility is but a picture (in the photographic sense of the word) taken of reality by our mind. (*La Pensée et le mouvant*, in *Oeuvres*, vol. III [Paris: Presses Universitaires de France, 1970], p. 560)

The direct intuition of living experience is more faithful to reality than conceptualizing (and thereby stabilizing) thought. Bergson contrasted psychological *duration* with physical *time*. Physical time is a mathematicized spatial concept based on the timeline analogy, while psychological duration is a creature of *experience* that functions in our thought-life where we encounter "succession without distinction . . . an interconnection and organization of elements, each one of which represents the whole, and cannot be distinguished or isolated from it except by [the distorting transformation of] abstract thought."[19] But the creative process typical of duration pervades nature and establishes the central role of change on the stage of natural existence. Everything in the world is caught up in a change of some sort, so that it is accurate rather than paradoxical to say that what is changing is change itself.

Nature is pervaded by a *nisus* or striving to bring to realization something more, something over and above the existing frame of things—and then is manifest with special force and vivacity in the organic realm where the creature forces of evolutionary development are pervasively at work. No two distinct stages of a thing and no two distinct experiences of it are ever exactly the same. Change, innovation, creativity are nature's essence and organic *life* in their most powerful expression. Evolution and *élan vital*—organic life's driving force of creative vitality—are everywhere at work. And this creativity and innovation are no mystery to us: We experience them in our own activities—above all, in our own acts of free will.[20]

Bergson substantially accepted Plato's approach to process. Both address the following aporetic cluster of individually plausible but collectively inconsistent contentions:

1. Only flux is experientially real; physical reality as we experience it is always unstable.
2. Adequate conceptual characterization of physical reality as we experience it is possible.
3. Concepts are always something fixed and stable.
4. Stable concepts cannot adequately characterize an unstable object.

Plato and Bergson alike resolve the inconsistency that arises here by rejecting 2 and denying that our concepts can capture physical reality. But they interpret the significance of this consideration differently. Plato effectively says, "So much the worse for experienced physical reality. Since *real* reality must be intelligible, this relegates the experienced physical realm to the status of a mere illusion." Bergson, by contrast, effectively says, "So much the worse for mere conceptual intelligibility. It reveals its own inadequacies by being unable to come to grips with experienced physical reality." For Bergson, the world transcends the limits of reason, seeing that a reality that has process, flux, and change as fundamental features cannot be adequately encompassed by any fixed set of descriptive categories.[21]

9. JOHN DEWEY (1859–1952)

The combination of pragmatism with processism at work in C. S. Peirce and William James is also found in the thought of John Dewey. It is particularly prominent in his 1920s lectures on James and Bergson. Like these thinkers, Dewey emphasized that experience is self-creation, citing with favor Bergson's example of "an artist standing before a blank canvas [who] puts up his brush, [and] no one—not even he himself—can know ahead of time what the result will be."[22] Dewey accordingly envisioned "an intrinsic connection of time with individuality" because "[individual] development cannot occur when an individual has power and capacities that are not actualized at a given time," although the potentialities at work are not Aristotelian ("connected to fixed, predestined ends") but rather open ended and novelty admitting:

> The career which is his unique individuality is the series of interactions in which he was created to be what he was by the ways in which he responded to the occasions with which he was presented. One cannot leave out either conditions *as opportunities* nor yet unique ways of responding to them. An occasion is an opportunity only when it is an evocation of a specific event, while a response is not a necessary effect of a cause but is a way of using an occasion to render it a constituent of an ongoing unique history. Individuality conceived as a temporal development involves uncertainty, indeterminacy, or contingency. Individuality is the source of whatever is unpredictable in the world.[23]

Like many processists, Dewey interpreted individuality and novelty in a way that takes human development to be the characteristic mode of innovative process.

As Dewey saw it, time and change constitute a mystery—the mystery of why and how "the world is as it is" that encompasses "the sense of development both creative and degenerative."[24] This mystery lies at the heart of the human situation in all its dimensions, social and intellectual alike: "The ground of democratic ideas and practices is found in the potentialities of individuals, in the capacity for positive developments if properly developed. . . . The free individuality which is the source of art is also the final source of creative development in time."[25]

With Dewey, as with James, there is a close relationship between processism and pragmatism. It was precisely because he saw human existence in terms of an emplacement within an environment of unstable flux that Dewey dismissed the prospect of governing life by rules and fixities, and saw the need of a flexible approach geared pragmatically to the changing demands of changing situations.[26]

10. ALFRED NORTH WHITEHEAD (1861–1947)

As indicated above, Whitehead has been the dominant figure in recent process philosophy.[27] Whitehead fixed on "process" as a central category of his philosophy because he, too—like James and Bergson before him—regarded time, change, and creativity as representing salient metaphysical factors. The building blocks of reality as envisioned in Whitehead's classic *Process and Reality* are not substances at all but "actual occasions"—processual units rather than "things" of some sort—with human experience affording their best analogon. Even as in conscious experience humans *apprehend* what goes on about them, so these actual activities "prehend" what goes on in their environment in a way that encompasses a low-grade mode of emotion, consciousness, and purpose. Thus Whitehead's "actual occasions" are, as it were, living units of elemental experience.

Whitehead saw two principal sorts of creative process at work in nature: those that are operative in shaping the internal make-up of a new concrete particular existent ("concretion") and those that are operative other-orientedly when existents function so as to bring new successors to realization ("transition"). But the "existents" at issue are not, of course, *substances* in the sense of old-line metaphysics but rather processual particulars ("actual occasions") of the aforementioned sort.

To be sure, Whitehead was first and foremost a geometer and, like Einstein, focused attention no less on space than on time. Still, invoking the name of Bergson, Whitehead adopted "Nature is a process" as a leading principle, and counted temporality, historicity, change, passage, and novelty among the most fundamental facts to be reckoned within our understanding of the world.[28] A unit of reality is "the ultimate creature derivative from the creative process," he remarked.[29] This view was underpinned by Whitehead's profound appreciation of Leibnizian *appetition*—the striving through which all things endeavor to bring new features to realization.[30] Like Leibniz, Whitehead did not see time as something independent of its existential content. For him, temporality and its changes are basic—a "perpetual perishing" matched by a perpetual emergence in the "concrescence" of new reals. And in back of this lay the Heraclitean doctrine that "all things flow" and the rejection of a Parmenidean/Atomistic view that nature consists in the changeable interrelations among stable, unchanging units of existence.[31]

In Whitehead, as in Leibniz, microcosm and macrocosm are coordinated, linked to one another in a seamless web of process. Whiteheadian entities, like Leibnizian monads, are infinitely complex and, in a way, boundless. Each represents a perspective on the world that reaches out to touch and, as it were, encompass the rest. In Whitehead, as in Leibniz, there is a dialectical tension between individual and world. Each item of existence in nature touches the others and without them would not be what it is. With Leibniz, Whitehead envisions a "philosophy of organism" in that everything that exists not only forms part of the organic organization of nature-as-a-whole but also will itself constitute an organism of sorts—an integrated whole with an organic constitution of its own. But it is the pervasiveness of the growth/decay cycle operative throughout nature that marks this metaphysic of organism as being a metaphysic of process as well. The conception of an experientially integrated whole—a unit that is an organically systemic whole—represents a line of thought that links Whitehead closely to Leibniz and Bergson.

Whitehead's metaphysical categories—experience, feeling, prehension, power and potentiality, organic activity, and development—all represent pivotal features of a philosophy of process. For him, novelty and innovation is ever the order of the day; as he saw it, the natural world is a sea of process. He emphatically rejected the idea of clear separations in nature:

There simply are no hard-edged objects with sharp-boundaried locations in space. He insisted that the traditional idea of "simple location" must be rejected; what we have in nature is a manifold of diffused processes spread out in a fieldlike manner over regions of space. (Clark Maxwell and the field approach in physics exerted a great influence on Whitehead and provided him with one of the principal paradigms of his thought.)

Moreover, with Whitehead, as with many of his contemporaries, the idea of evolution played a key role. He saw the evolution of living organisms on earth as a particular manifestation of the most fundamental creative process of the universe in general. It is not directed by laws beyond itself but generated from large populations of entities all at once seeking their own fulfillment and contributing, over countless generations, to the great cycle of generational succession that makes for the advance of the whole. Evolution is of course not a thing, of some kind, but the name we give a process consisting in the ongoing succession of dynamic elements, each maturing its transitory contribution to the unfolding of existence. And time, like evolution, is also not a thing but the name we give to overall series of risings and perishings of concrete moments of satisfaction and sacrifice. Time is therefore fundamentally the byproduct of "enjoyment" (as Whitehead called it, stretching the term to its limits).

Strongly opposed to sharp divisions and dichotomies of all kinds, Whitehead condemned "the bifurcation of nature." For him, the world is an organic whole that exhibits a unified fabric in which all threads are linked together. Whitehead takes a prismatic view of reality: All existence is multiply many-faceted, and existence at all levels, from subatomic to cosmic, exhibits physical, organic, intellectual (infraction-processing), and axiological (normative/evaluative) characteristics.

In theory, one can have a process philosophy that is oriented phenomenologically (in seeing process as fundamental in human experience and in the order of cognition), or biologically (in seeing process as fundamental in life and in the order of organic existence), or physicalistically (in seeing process as fundamental in nature and in the order of physical existence).

But in Whitehead, the most thoroughgoing processist of recent times, all three of these approaches are unhesitatingly fused into a seamless whole.[32] He saw the real as prismatic, as contriving all those different facets conjointly. The amplitude of Whitehead's thought is demonstrated by the extent to which its speculative dimension can be linked to current trends in continental philosophy and conjointly the extent to which its processual doctrines can be linked to the concerns of analytic philosophy.[33]

Whitehead's influence on the development and diffusion of process philosophy was immense—indeed, decisive. His challenging writings, his many years of teaching at Harvard, and the force of his example as a scientifically literate philosopher combined to make for a widely sympathetic reception of his ideas. One recent historian rightly says that "it was not strange that for many professional philosophers he became not merely a major thinker with whom dialogue was possible but even something of a cult figure."[34]

11. WILMON H. SHELDON (1875–1981)

W. H. Sheldon, who studied at Harvard and taught for many years at Yale, stands prominently among the earlier American process philosophers whose work proceeded in substantial independence from Whitehead.[35] He, too, opposed—quite independently—what Whitehead called the "bifurcation of nature" and rejected the various dualisms that had figured so prominently in the history of philosophy. The real, according to Sheldon, exhibits in all of its aspects an active, ever-fluctuating intermediation between various polar opposites (being/nonbeing, stability/change, activity/passivity, etc.). As he saw it, such ambivalent fluctuation operates throughout nature, forever averting the stable fixity of an unyielding extreme. No destructive conflict, but a productive advance, is marked in such tensions. For process, in its role as an active motor of change from A to B, thereby also links and unites A and B into a connected and integrated whole. "The role of the principle of process is to remove the clash and conflict between [such] polar opposites. . . . Process comes in to help out polarity, and in doing so helps itself also."[36] Sheldon encapsulates this idea in a principle of "productive duality," which holds that reality—like Zeno's flying arrow—encompasses and unites through a "sameness in difference" *both* the fixity of a definite position *and* the transiency of a continual change.[37]

In particular, Sheldon saw the conflict of philosophical systems—materialism vs. idealism, intellectualism vs. voluntarism, determinism vs. indeterminism, and so on—as products of failure to realize the existence of productive polar tensions through the distorting overemphasis on one of two interconnected polar opposites. For him, the situation of electromagnetism is paradigmatic: The real phenomena we confront are one and all products of a creative opposition of polar opposites.[38] These opposites do not cancel each other out but create a tension or destabilization that gives rise to process of development. The result of opposition is thus not neutralization but a tension that engenders processual change.

Unlike Bergson or James, Sheldon saw Zeno's puzzles not so much as paradoxes but as signposts toward the solution of a productive duality in indicating how reality transcends the limits of a static analysis. Through its unstable, productive, and creative nature, reality resists the fixity with which we humans endow it through a language-inherent overemphasis on some aspect. The processual nature of the real enables it to transcend the spurious conflicts and incompatibilities engendered by a human myopia that inheres in our reliance for fixed and stable conceptual classifiers. In a manner reminiscent of the Egg of Columbus, Sheldon dismisses the logicians' quibbles with the splendid dictum "Reality solves its own problems in the very act of existing."[39]

12. RETROSPECT

The teachings of these various exponents of process philosophy illustrate the fertile variety of ideas and doctrines that this approach has manifested over the years. However greatly these positions differ in other regards (and they do so enormously), they all agree in seeing time, process, change, and

historicity as among the fundamental categories for understanding the real. They put into focus the point, duly emphasized by Whitehead himself, that process philosophy does not
represent the position of any particular thinker but reflects a
major tendency or line of thought that traces back through
the history of philosophy to the days of the Pre-Socratics. Nor
did this philosophical approach come to an end with the work
of this eminent exponent; it was continued not only by his
school (including Charles Hartshorne and Paul Weiss, among
others) but also by other philosophers of different allegiance.[40]

After all, no philosophical position as such is *defined* by
its historical exponents; it is at most *exemplified* by them.
And, in fact, the process-oriented approach in metaphysics is
historically too pervasive and systematically too significant to
be restricted in its bearing to one particular philosopher and
his adherents. Indeed, one important task for the partisans of
process at this particular juncture of philosophical history is
to prevent the idea of "process philosophy" from being margin-
alized through a limitation of its bearing to the work and influence of any one single individual or narrowly defined school,
however prominent. Indeed, the historical process of process
philosophy's own development instantiates and vividly illus-
trates process philosophy's message that we live in a world
where nothing stands still and that change is of the very
essence of reality.

The process approach has been a particularly important
development in and for American philosophy—especially
owing to its increasingly close linkage to pragmatism in such
thinkers as Peirce, James, and Dewey. In recent decades, the
great majority of its principal exponents have done their philosophical work in the United States, and it is here that interest
in this approach to philosophy has been the most intense and
extensive, constituting a considerable subsector within
American philosophy at large. To be sure, philosophy in North
America is too complex and diversified an enterprise to be
captured or even dominated by any one school of thought; it
is a highly diversified manifold that encompasses tendencies
of thought representing a wide variety of sources. There is no
question, however, that process thought constitutes one

(albeit only one) very prominent sector of the active philosophical scene in the United States at the present time. Apart from
the proliferation of books and articles on the topic,[41] other
indicators of this phenomenon include the formation of the
Society for Process Studies, as well as the prominence of
process philosophizing under the aegis of the Society for
American Philosophy and the American Metaphysical Society.
Another clear token is the journal *Process Studies*, published
by the Center for Process Studies in Claremont, California,
and founded in 1971 by Lewis S. Ford and John B. Cobb, Jr.,
a publication that has in recent years become a major vehicle
for article-length discussions in the field. Representatives of
process philosophy occupy influential posts in departments of
philosophy and religious studies in many of America's univer-
sities and colleges, and some half-dozen doctoral dissertations
are produced annually in this field. American philosophy is at
this historic juncture an agglomeration of different industries,
and process philosophy is prominent among them.

Regrettably, authors of histories and surveys not infre-
quently fail to give process philosophy the recognition that is
its due. For example, the otherwise excellent survey of
American philosophy by the able French scholar Gerard
Deledalle omits all mention of process philosophy as such and
takes only perfunctory notice of Whitehead in an appendix.[42]
To take the line is not, perhaps, to give us *Hamlet* without the
ghost, but is at least tantamount to omitting Horatio.

From the days of the Pyrrhonian sceptics of antiquity we
are told again and again throughout the history of philosophy
that speculative systematization is inappropriate—that such
knowledge as we humans can actually obtain is confined to
the realm of everyday life and/or its precisification through
science. Repeated in every era, this stricture is also rejected by
many within each. The impetus for big-picture understanding,
for a coherent and panoramic view of things that puts the var-
iegated bits and pieces together, represents an irrepressible
demand of the human intellect as a possession of "the rational
animal." And process metaphysics affords one of the most
promising and serious options for accommodating this
demand.

2

Basic Ideas

SYNOPSIS

(1, 2) The characteristic feature of process philosophy is its stress on the primacy of activity—and on the range of associated factors such as time, change, innovation, and so forth. It maintains that these conceptions are not just necessary but even basic to our understanding of the world. (3) The conception of a process is complex: It combines the features of internal make-up with change and development in time. (4) The idea of process is subject to various fundamental distinctions, especially productive/ transformative and owned/unowned. (5) Process philosophy does not—or need not—deny substances (things), but sees them as subordinate in status and ultimately inhering in processes. Moreover, process philosophy stresses the reality and prominence of literally autonomous, *altogether unowned processes that do not merely represent the activities of substances. It thus rejects the* Process Reducibility Thesis *that all processes reduce to the actions of things. (6) A fundamental feature of the real is that it is processual in nature, and the only ultimately satisfactory way to understand what things* are *is to proceed in terms of what they* do.

1. The Process Approach and Its Alternatives

Process philosophy has two closely interrelated sectors, the one conceptual or epistemic and the other metaphysical or ontological. The conceptual aspect is based on the idea that process and its ramifications affords the most appropriate and effective conceptual instruments for understanding the world we live in. And the ontological aspect inheres in the idea that this conceptual state of affairs obtains because process is the most pervasive, characteristic, and crucial feature of reality. This duality of doctrinal perspective leads to there being two distinct (albeit compatible) versions of process philosophy. In its stronger version, process philosophy is an *ontological* reductionism that sees all physical things as reducible to physical processes. In its weaker version, process philosophy is a *conceptual* reductionism that sees the explanation of the idea of a "thing" as necessarily involving a recourse to processual ideas. Process philosophy thus has both an ontological and a conceptual side, and process philosophers differ in the respective emphasis that they give to one or the other. (The mixed—and thereby more complicated—option of a theory of things-in-process has not found much favor since the hey-day of Aristotelianism.)

As process philosophers see it, the supposed predominance and permanence of "things" in nature is at best a useful fiction and at worst a misleading delusion. "Material objects" are ultimately comprised of energy that is in an ongoing state of flux and motion. All those supposedly constant things that seem to maintain a continuous identity through the vicissitudes of time and change are, in fact, little more than loci of comparative (and transitory) stability within a manifold of continual change, engaged in an inexorable transit leading from birth through maturation to decline and destruction. Thus, in general terms, process philosophy is predicated on two contentions:

- In a dynamic world, *things* cannot do without *processes.* Since substantial things change, their nature must encompass some impetus to internal development.
- In a dynamic world, *processes* are more fundamental than *things.* Since substantial things emerge in and from the world's course of changes, processes have priority over things.

Becoming and change—the origination, flourishing, and passing of the old and the innovative emergence of ever-new existence—constitute the central themes of process metaphysics.

The standpoint of process philosophy goes against the grain of much Western metaphysics, which has generally exhibited a marked bias in favor of *things*. Aristotle's insistence on the primacy of substance and its ramifications (see *Metaphysics* IV, 2, 1003b6–11)—with its focus on midsize physical objects on the order of a rock, a tree, a cat, or a human being—has proved to be decisive for much of Western philosophy. Process metaphysics, however, has deliberately chosen to reverse this perspective. It insists on seeing process as basic in the order of being or at least of understanding. We cannot adequately describe (let alone explain) processes in terms of something nonprocessual any more than we can describe (or explain) spatial relation in nonspatial terms of reference. The processual order is, in this sense, conceptually closed.[1]

One of the main supports of this reversal of perspective lies in the inescapable fact that process is pervasive both in nature and in human affairs. Natural and human history is commonly regarded as a collection of notable events—the separation of the moon from the earth, say, or the extinction of dinosaurs or the assassination of Abraham Lincoln. But, of course, when any one of these "events" is examined in detail, it soon becomes clear that, in fact, a long and complicated *process* is involved, a sequence of activities and transactions that in each case constitutes an elaborate story of interconnected developments. On closer inspection, the idea of discrete "events" dissolves into a manifold of processes which themselves dissolve into further processes.

And what holds for discrete *events* holds also for discrete *things*. For while Western metaphysics has generally favored things over processes, another variant line of thought was also current from the earliest times onward. After all, the concentration on perduring physical *things* as existents in nature slights the equally good claims of another ontological category, namely, *processes, activities, events, occurrences*—items better indicated by verbs than nouns. Clearly, storms and heat waves are every bit as real as dogs and oranges. Even on the surface of it, verb-entities have as good a claim to reality as noun-entities. For process theorists, *becoming* is no less important than *being*—but rather the reverse. *How* eventuations transpire is seen as no less significant than *what* sorts of things are involved. The phenomenology of change is stressed by processists precisely because the difference between a static museum and the real world of vibrant activity is emblematic of our understanding of reality. Process philosophers accordingly reject the stance of an exaggeratedly idealistic theory of temporality that takes time and its works to lie wholly in the eyes of the beholder. (Indeed, they take the very dynamism of changing beholdings to betoken an indispensable role for time that precludes its exile from the explanatory order.)

Processes can, in fact, accomplish the job usually assigned to substance by philosophers. And any of the characterizations of substances in the ontological tradition will, in fact, hold good of particular processes:

> *Spinoza:* By *substance* I understand that what is in itself and is conceived through itself; in other words, that the conception of which does not need the conception of another thing from which it must be formed. (*Ethics*, Bk. I, Def. 3)

> *Wolff:* A subject that can perdure and be modified is called a *substance*. (*Philosophia Prima sive Ontologia*, para. 768)

> *Kant:* The schema of substance is permanence of the real in time, that is, the representation of empirical determinations of time in general, and so as abiding while all else changes. (*CPuR*, B 183)

> *Hegel:* Substance is . . . [that which] maintains itself as One in the interplay of actualities. (*Encyclopedia of Philosophy*, para. 97)

It is clear that many such substance-characterizations, and numerous others found in the classical literature, will ultimately hold true every bit as much for processes as for the material objects that are usually regarded as the paradigm substances or things.

Much metaphysical dispute and disagreement exhibits a fundamentally evaluative character in that it turns less on what might be called the discernible facts of the matter than on the assessment of their importance. The key issues are ones of significance, centrality, priority, and emphasis. And in this regard, the position of process metaphysics is that the interests of a just appreciation of the world's realities call for prioritizing

- activity over substance
- process over product
- change over persistence
- novelty over continuity

Seen in this perspective, process philosophy does not—or need not—deny the reality and validity of the second members of these pairs but rather maintains that in the order of significance they must be subordinated to the first. It is the issue of the comparative priority or importance as regards being or at least understanding that is the bone of contention.

Accordingly, "process philosophy" is best understood as a doctrine committed, or at any rate inclined, to certain basic teachings or contentions:

- that time and change are among the principal categories of metaphysical understanding
- that process is a principal category of ontological description
- that processes—and the force, energy, and power that they make manifest—are more fundamental, or at any rate not less fundamental, than things for the purposes of ontological theory
- that several if not all of the major elements of the ontological repertoire (God, nature-as-a-whole, persons, material substances) are best understood in process terms
- that contingency, emergence, novelty, and creativity are among the fundamental categories of metaphysical understanding.

A process philosopher, then, is someone for whom such processes are metaphysically pivotal, someone for whom temporality, activity, and change—of alteration, striving, passage, and novelty emergence—are the ontologically, or at least hermeneutically, most salient dimension of the real. Ultimately it is a question of primacy—of viewing the time-bound aspects of the real as constituting its most characteristic and significant features. For the process philosopher, process has priority over product in the order of being or at least of understanding.

Process philosophy issues an invitation to accept the world's arrangements in their full complexity. Its acknowledgment of fundamentally different kinds of processes inclines process philosophy against materialism. For if there indeed are different and distinct processual modes, why should one feel any compulsion to reduce some to others—the mental to the physical as with traditional materialism, say, or the symbolic to the material as with traditional nominalism?

However, process metaphysics is not, in the final analysis, so much a doctrine as a tendency—a mode of approach to the philosophical issues. It can be developed in very different directions, varying with the question of what sort of process one takes to be paradigmatic or fundamental. If it is a mechanical or physical process, one sort of doctrine results (a materialism of some sort), while if it is mental or psychical, a very different sort of doctrine results (an idealism of some description). If a single sort of process is basic, we have a monism, while if a pluralism of fundamental processes is envisioned, then a metaphysical pluralism will emerge. Process metaphysics as such is doctrinal tendency rather than a concrete position. And it can even issue in substantially naturalistic doctrine if, at the metaphysical level, one regards the world as a congeries of highly diversified but interrelated natural processes, leaving the details to be worked out by the positive (natural) sciences. (Nothing in principle prevents process metaphysics from taking a predominantly empiricistic and naturalistic line.)

Accordingly, process philosophy is best seen as a broad movement that urges a particular sort of approach to the problems of metaphysics—a general strategy to the description and explanation of the real. However, while process philosophy is a generalized approach rather than a unified doctrine, it does, nevertheless, involve a certain doctrinal tendency or inclination, namely, to see substantial things as subordinate to processes both ontologically (in the order of being) and conceptually (in the order of understanding).

Mario Bunge has said that one should dismiss "the quaint version of process metaphysics that dispenses with the thing concept, because it is logically untenable; indeed it is circular to define a thing as the collection of events occurring in it," seeing that that "it" must refer to the thing at issue.[2] But this otherwise sensible observation invites two comments. First, the process metaphysician has no wish (and no need) for dispensing with the thing *concept*—indeed, it would be difficult to articulate the position at issue without making use of the concept. Metaphysics after all is not a battle over *concepts* as such but rather of their significance. Second, what process metaphysics wishes to do is to argue that the items we categorize as "things" (as ordinarily understood) are more instructively and adequately understood as instantiations of certain sorts of process or process-complexes.

To be sure, process philosophers are not promoting a reformation or transformation of ordinary language. Nobody seriously proposes that instead of speaking of "yonder flower" one should speak of "yonder florescent process" or instead of speaking of "this pen" one should speak of "this instance of a pen process." This is no more at issue than the chemist insisting on asking a waiter for a glass of H_2O or the worried pet owner asking the veterinarian about the health of his *Felix domesticus*. The person interested in achieving theoretical precision is not (or need not be) carrying the torch of linguistic reform. Copernicans have not desisted from speaking of sunrises. Process philosophy is concerned with modes of understanding, not modes of discourse. Process philosophers have no compunction about retaining substance terms and concepts, and do not propose dispensing with them in favor of an exclusively processual vocabulary; rather, they insist that such terms are *in principle* reducible to process talk (stronger version) or at least represent a more informative mode of understanding things (weaker version).

As is often the case in philosophy, the position at issue in process philosophy is best understood in terms of what it opposes. And this, like so much else in the field, takes us back to the ancient Greeks. One school of philosophers strikingly committed to the primacy of substances were the Greek atomists of pre-Socratic times. As they saw it, atoms were unchanging units of existence, defined as such simply by the possession of certain unchanging factors (qualities), namely, their shape (configuration) and size. The only change which such atoms admit is one of their relative spatial distribution in relation to one another—so that every sort of natural process is, in the final analysis, reducible to the activities (i.e., the movements) of substances (atoms). The only sort of process in the world is thus one of the motion of atoms—their change of position. And all other changes are reducible to this—to the reshuffling of the positions of otherwise unchanging atoms in their placement relationships to one another within the vast spatial matrix that embraces them all alike (the "void"). And since the rearrangement of atoms is all there is, the world's overall condition is at bottom always uniformly the same. Progress, advance, development—in short, teleology in all its forms—have no place in nature's scheme of things. No ontological doctrine could be more emphatic regarding the ontological primacy of stable substances than Greek atomism, which, for this very reason, is the quintessence of everything to which process philosophy is opposed.

2. KEY CONCEPTS AND CATEGORIES

The idea of process represents what might be called a *categorial* concept—one that provides a thought-instrument for organizing the knowledge afforded us by our experience of the world's course of events.[3] For process metaphysics, the overarching neutral category of *existent item* or *entity* or *individual* branches out into two realizations: *things* (substances) and *processes* (activities). And the second of these offers a smoother journey.

Process metaphysics is really less of a theory than a point of view taking the line that one must prioritize processes over things and activities over substances. Accordingly, a process metaphysic propounds certain characteristic stresses of emphasis in contrast to those of a substance metaphysic, as follows:

Substance Philosophy	*Process Philosophy*
discrete individuality	interactive relatedness
separateness	wholeness (totality)
condition (fixity of nature)	activity (self-development)
uniformity of nature	innovation/novelty
unity of being	unity of law
(individualized specificity)	(functional typology)
descriptive fixity	productive energy, drive, etc.
classificatory stability	fluidity and evanescence
passivity (being acted upon)	activity (agency)

Process philosophy thus prioritizes change and development in all of its aspects over fixity and persistence.

The crux of the process/substance controversy lies in the distinction between *occurrences* and *things*. Mainstream ontologists have in general endowed things with the permanence of perduring substances over time, supposing that things remain self-identical through time on the basis of their possession of certain essential features or properties that remain changelessly intact across temporal changes. Accordingly, the problem of substance ontology has always been that it is somewhere between difficult and impossible to specify any such change-exempt descriptive properties or nonclassificating features that stably characterize the essence of things. Process philosophy frees itself from this difficulty by simply averting the problem.

The theoretical approach that is characteristic of process philosophy is clearly indicated in the contrast between its own schedule of ontological categories and those of the traditional Aristotelian scheme (see Display 1). One theorist quite appropriately observes: "Process philosophers disagree as to which categories deserve emphasis. Thus Dewey stressed situation;

Hartshorne, sociality; Bergson time; and Ushenko, power."[4]
But such differences of emphasis do not militate against a
basic consensus on the fundamental issues.

DISPLAY 1

Aristotle's Categories	Process Categories
substance	process
quantity	quantitative features
quality	topicality (thematic nature)
relation	relationships (interconnections)
place/space and time	spatiotemporal location
state	(inner) condition/structure, order, situation
action and affection	force, energy, change, power; causal antecedence and consequence
possession	accompaniments ("social order")

Note: Exactly the same range of questions (what, on what scale, of
what sort, etc. are answered on both sides, but in each case relative
to their own characteristically different frame of reference.

Yet is it not unfaithful to the spirit of process philosophy
to propound any stable set of categories at all?[5] Should a philosophy that sees everything as being in process not reject the
idea of a fixed category scheme?

The resolution of this problem lies in the fact that—as the
display indicates—categories relate to *questions* and not to
answers: they deal with *what, where, when, how,* and the
like. Categories by their very nature are problem oriented. And
process philosophy has no quarrel with there being (at least
some) permanent questions; what it rejects are permanent
solutions. At the most abstract level of generality—though
only there—our questions remain the same (what, on what
scale, of what sort, where-and-when, etc.), though, of course,
the details are ever-changing in the course of cognitive progress, as are the answers. And so categorical uniformity (on

the side of abstract, high-level questions) is not at odds with processual variability (on the side of substantial detail). Moreover, process is a natural categorical resort, because we humans understand change owing to the fact that we *experience* change in ourselves: We act or do things, and things happen to us. Human agency as we experience it qualifies as paradigmatic for process, because—like instructions for swimming or broad jumping—what is involved is a programmed sequence of actions or activities.

Process thinkers thus favor the idea of macroprocesses that organize microprocesses into systemic wholes. The idea of system has ever been prominent in their thought, with organic, biological systems as a paradigm. Deeply rooted in the philosophy of Aristotle, this idea has figured prominently throughout process philosophy from Leibniz to Bergson and Whitehead. Leibniz may speak here for the whole tradition:

> [The] interlinkage or accommodation of all created things to each other, and of each to all others, brings it about that each simple substance has relations that express all the others, and is in consequence a perpetual living mirror of the universe, [In nature] all is a plenum, which renders all matter interconnected, and as in a plenum any motion has some effect on distant bodies in proportion to their distance—so that each body is affected not only by those that touch it, in some way feeling the effects of all that happens to them, but also through their mediation feeling affected by those in contact with the former by which it is directly touched—it follows that this inter-communication extends to any distance, however great. And in consequence, all bodies feel the effects of everything that happens in the universe. (*Monadology*, sects. 56 & 61)

Ever since Aristotle's day, process thought has been closely linked to biological conceptions. An animal—or human being, for that matter—can be conceived of either as an assembly of conjoined physical components (feet, arms, head, etc.) or as a unified manifold of interrelated functional systems (alimentary system, circulatory system, sensory system, nervous system, etc.): It can be thought of in terms of parts or in terms of processes. And it is pretty clear, even on the surface of it, that the latter, functional approach provides for a more helpful explanation of what such a creature is all about. On this basis, process philosophy has generally adapted such an organismic approach, inclining to see the world's constituents in the light of biological analogies, as organically integrated systems of coordinated processes. Accordingly, Leibniz, Bergson, and Whitehead (to take only three outstanding examples) are all metaphysicians whose processism is closely geared to an organicist approach.

3. WHAT IS A PROCESS?

It is profitable to examine more closely exactly what a process is. A process is a coordinated group of changes in the complexion of reality, an organized family of occurrences that are systematically linked to one another either causally or functionally. It is emphatically not necessarily a change in or of an individual thing, but can simply relate to some aspect of the general "condition of things." A process consists in an integrated series of connected developments unfolding in conjoint coordination in line with a definite program. Processes are correlated with occurrences or events: Processes always involve various events, and events exist only in and through processes.

Processes develop over time. Even as there can be no instantaneous wail or drought, so there is no such thing as an instantaneous process. Processes will always involve a variety of subordinate processes and events, even as the process of creating a book involves its writing, production, and distribution. And processes almost inevitably involve not just perdurance and continuity but also change over time. Even mere attention varies with the passage of time, as William James noted when he likened consciousness to "a bird's life; it seems to be made of an alternation of flights and perchings."[6] Moreover, just as the static complexity of a set of (filmstrip-like) photographs of a flying arrow does not adequately capture its dynamic motion, so the conjunctive complexity of a process's description does not adequately capture its transtemporal dynamics.

Owing to the programmatic nature of what is involved, it is of the very essence of an ongoing process that it combines existence in the present with tentacles reaching into the past and the future. A natural process is not a mere collection of sequential presents but inherently exhibits a structure of spatiotemporal continuity.[7] A natural process by its very nature passes on to the future a construction made from the materials of the past.

The successive stages of a natural process are not a mere juxtaposition of arbitrary, unconnected factors (like passengers assembled by mere chance in a ship or plane). They are united by a systemic causal or functional agency under the aegis of a lawful regularity—even as in language use the letters of a word or the words of a sentence are limited not just by arbitrary juxtaposition but by ordering principles that forge these sequences into meaningful semantical units. The unity of a process is the unity of a lawful order that need not be fully determinative but is at least delimitative.

But how can a process preserve its own self-identity in the face of alteration—how it can be one particular item and yet change? The answer lies in a single factor: internal complexity. A process does not change as such—as the particular overall process at issue—but any such process can incorporate change through its unifying amalgamation of stages or phases (which may themselves be processes). Even as a story can encompass foolishness without itself being foolish, so a process can encompass changes without itself changing.

All processes have a developmental, forward-looking aspect. Each envisions some sector of the future and canalizes it into regions of possibility more restrained in range than would otherwise, in theory, be available. The inherent futurition of process is an exfoliation of the real by successively actualizing possibilities that are cast aside as so many useless husks as the process unfolds.

Since Whitehead, and indeed since Boscovitch, the concept of physical (gravitational or electromagnetic) field has been an important paradigm for process philosophy. The process philosopher has replaced a *horror vacui* with a *horror separationis*, being impelled by the paradoxes of Zeno into the conviction that once reality falls apart into disjointed discreteness, not all the king's horses and all the king's men can get it together again. (The "fuzzy" character of the real is a key theme of Bergson and James.) The contribution of the process idea is to help us to keep together in function things that thought inclines to separate in idea.

How are instantiations of a generally identical process to be reidentified? What is it that makes "this first typing of AND" and "this second typing of AND" two instances of the same process? Obviously it is not the sameness of the product— otherwise indistinguishable ANDs can, in principle, be produced in very different ways by very different processes. Rather, structural identity of operation is the crux: The two concrete processes involved are simply two different spatiotemporal instances of the same generic production procedure—that is, the same general recipe is followed in either case.

A particular process is (by hypothesis) a fixed sort of eventuation sequence. But this, of course, does not stand in the way of innovation. On one hand, there is the emergence of new processes that have not been instantiated before. On the other hand, there is the novel concatenation of old micro-processes into new macroprocesses—the combination of old processes into new processual structures.

Identifiable processes generally have their ordinary course of programmatic development, but this is not inexorable, and its unfolding can be blocked by uncooperative developments. Things can go wrong and the normal unfolding of a process can be aborted through the intrusion of external developments, as when the germination and growth of the acorn into an oak tree is aborted through its being eaten by a passing pig or through circumstances that lead to its being deprived of water or of light.

A process is made into the item it is not through its continuing ("essential") properties, as with a classically conceived substance, but by its history, by the temporal structure of its descriptive unfolding across time. The identity of a process is constituted through a sequential pattern of action: Its *ending* is *its* ending because it is joined with what goes before as part of a characteristic program of occurrence. To be sure, the programming of a process need not be totally deterministic—it can leave room for some degree of inner looseness—of variation and alternative possibilities. (For instance, a young girl's development through adolescence and puberty into adult womanhood is a definite process but does not take exactly the same detailed course in every case.) The basic idea of process involves the unfolding of a characterizing program through determinate stages. The concept of programmatic (rule-conforming) developments is definitive of the idea of process: The unity/identity of a process is the unity/identity of its program. If the "connection" at issue in that "sequence of *connected* developments" is one of actual causality, then we have a *physical* process; if it is mental or mathematical operations, then we have process of different sorts. However, for present purposes, it is the physical processes that constitute the natural world about us which will be the focus of concern.

4. Modes of Process

The key distinction between *productive* and *transformative* processes may be set out as follows:

- *product-productive processes* that produce actual products that can themselves be characterized as things or substances (for example, manufacturing processes that produce pencils or automobiles, seed germinations that produce plants)
- *state-transformative processes* that merely transform states of affairs in general, paving the way for further processes without issuing in particular things or states thereof (for example, windstorms or earthquakes).

This distinction is important for present purposes because process philosophy is characterized by its insistence on the fundamentality of transformative processes, with their potential detachment from substantial things.

The distinction between *owned* and *unowned* processes also plays an important role in process philosophy. Owned processes are those that represent the activity of agents: the chirping of birds, the flowering of a bush, the rotting of a fallen tree. Such processes are ownership attributable with respect to "substantial" items. Unowned processes, by contrast, are free floating, as it were, and do not represent the activity of actual (i.e., more than nominal) agents: the cooling of the temperature, the change in climate, the flashing of lightning, the fluctuation of a magnetic field. From the process philosopher's point of view, the existence of unowned processes is particularly important because it shows that the realm of process as a whole is something additional to and separable from the realm of substantial things.

One of the most important ways of classifying processes is by the thematic nature of the operations at issue. On this basis we would have (for example) the distinction between processes of the following kinds:

- physical causality (in relation to physical changes)
- purposive/teleological (in relation to achieving deliberate objectives)
- cognitive/epistemic (in relation to intellectual problem solving—e.g., programming ourselves for solving a certain sort of problem)
- communicative (in relation to transmitting information)

These processual distinctions are among some of the most important in the domain, though of course they do not exhaust the subject. The taxonomy of processes is a complex and diversified venture, and the present indications do no more than make a start, with the distinction between physical and mental processes playing a role of particular importance.

5. THE PRIORITY OF PROCESS:
AGAINST THE PROCESS REDUCIBILITY THESIS

For Whitehead—as for the Schopenhauer of *The World as Will and Idea* (*Wille und Vorstellung*) and the Leibniz of *percep-*

tion theory before him—human experience constitutes the model or ideal type of the processes that characterize natural reality in general. For Whitehead saw the core nature of reality as typified by the living experience of an "actual occasion" arrayed in its full subjective immediacy. But perhaps this experience-as-paradigm mode of processism goes a bit too far; perhaps instead of seeing natural process as enfeebled experience, we should—inversely—see human experience as a quintessential and peculiarly vivid sort of natural process. The difference here may look, on first sight, as one of emphasis alone, but is in fact one of fundamental principle, because it shows that a plausible processism need not necessarily be anthropomorphic, as so much of process philosophy has actually been. There are—or certainly can be—kinds of natural processes entirely beyond the realm of human experience. (In fact, even if one takes human experience as one's paradigmatic explanatory analogy-model for the concept of a process—as processists from Leibniz to Whitehead generally do—one need not endorse an assimilation of *ontological* kind here, conceptual analogy being one sort of thing and ontological kinship another.)

From process philosophy's point of view, this question of the role of experience as a paradigm of process has an importance that transcends the mere splitting of explanatory hairs. For all experience is *owned*: every experience is somebody's experience. But processes, as we have seen, are not necessarily owned: Not every process can be seen as consisting, in the final analysis, in the activities of one or more things. Thus, if experience were to make good its claims to primacy here, this would, in a way, compromise the fundamentality of process by putting *owned* processes (of a certain sort) into a position of primacy.

Let us explore this aspect of the matter somewhat more deeply. Following Aristotle, the medieval schoolmen espoused the principle *Operari sequitur esse*. As they saw it, operation (process) is subordinate to the being of things; all actually is the activity of substantial things, so that every process is *owned*. Process philosophy of course rejects this position. Indeed, it effectively reverses this priority principle. Its motto is

Esse sequitur operari: things are constituted out of the flow of process, and substantiality is subordinate to activity. Things simply are what they do. As process philosophers see it, processes are basic and things derivative—not least because it takes a mental process (of a separation and individuation) to extract "things" from the blooming buzzing confusion of the world's physical processes. And so while substance metaphysics sees processes as manifesting dispositions that are themselves products of the categorical (nondispositional) features of things, process metaphysics involves an inversion of this perspective. It takes the line that the categorical properties of things are simply stable clusters of process-engendering dispositions.

Thus, consider the following Process Reducibility Thesis:

> The only sorts of processes there are are *owned* processes—processes that represent the doings of substances. There just are no processes apart from those that constitute the activity of identifiable agents. All process is reducible to the doings of (nonprocessual) things.

On the approach of such a substantialistic processism, it is conceded that nature is indeed replete with many and varied activities and processes but insisted that they are simply the doings of substantial agents. Every verb must have a subject and every event or occurrence is a matter of the agency of things. Denying the ontological autonomy of processes, this process-reducibility doctrine insists that all there is in the world are things and their properties and actions. Traditional metaphysics is inclined to view processes (such as the rod's snapping under the strain when bent sufficiently) as the manifestation of dispositions (fragility) which are themselves rooted in the stable properties of things.

This substantialism is an eminently implausible position. For while *some* processes do indeed consist in the activities of things (the ticking of the clock), nevertheless many other processes are emphatically *not* this sort. And with all such *unowned* and, as it were, autonomous processes, we clearly have processes that do not involve the properties or actions of things but rather reflect changes in nonsubstantial powers, fields, agencies, conditions, and circumstances. It would be very mistaken to think that only substance-coordinated processes exist. For it must be stressed that processes do not necessarily involve the doings of substantial *things*. The fire's heat causes the water to boil. But it is clearly not a *thing*. To be sure, some events and processes relate to the doings or undergoings of things (the collapse of the bridge) or of people (Smith's falling asleep). And other events and processes relate to the coordinated doings of things (an eclipse of the sun) or of people (a traffic jam). But many events and processes are patently subjectless in that they do not consist of the doings of one or more personal or impersonal agents. (A frost, for example, or the spread of a rumor and the vibrancy of a magnetic field.) What is at work in these self-subsistent or subjectless processes are not "agents" but "forces." And these can be diffusely located (the Renaissance) or, indeed, lack any specific physical location at all (the increase of the world's entropy over time). The fact is that we are surrounded on all sides by all sorts of phenomena more easily conceived of as processes than as substantial things—not only physical items like a magnetic field or an aurora borealis, but also conceptual artifacts like words and letters of the alphabet, let alone songs, plays, and poems.

A nomic (or law-governed) domain is one where events issue lawfully from the realization of certain conditions or states of affairs. The processes of any such a realm or world involve the realizations of dispositions all right, but not necessarily of the dispositions of *things*. For, in principle, *states of affairs*—which may simply be process complexes—can also provide the ontological support of dispositions. Actual substances simply need not be at issue.

After all, the world is full of processes that do not represent the action of things (save on a primitive and obsolescent atomist/materialistic model of nature). The idea that processes *can* be the doings of things represents a plain truth. But the idea that processes *must* be the doings of things is nothing but an unhelpful prejudice. The fluctuations of an electromagnetic field or the erosion of the shoreline are instances of processes that are not really the machinations of identifiable "things." Such processes can leave an impact on things (magnetic needles, for example). But by no stretch of the imagination are these processes themselves the doings/activities of things/ substances. There is clearly not such a *thing* as "a magnetic field" or "a gravitational field" that *does* something or *performs* certain actions. (And where is the thing that is being active when we have a fall in barometric pressure?)

Not that process metaphysics is ex officio compelled to reject "substantial" things! Rather, it has the convenient option of seeing them themselves in processual terms. For the paradigmatic process metaphysician, substance (thing) and property (attribute) are relational and processual in nature. To be a substance (thing-unit) is to function as a thing-unit in various situations. And to *have* a property is to *exhibit* this property in various contexts. (The only fully independent substances are those which—like people—self-consciously *take* themselves to be units.)

As far as process philosophy is concerned, things can be conceptualized as clusters of actual and potential processes. With Kant, the process philosopher wants to identify what a thing *is* with what it *does* (or, at any rate, can do). After all, even on the basis of an ontology of substance and property, processes are *epistemologically* fundamental. Without them, a thing is inert, undetectable, disconnected from the world's causal commerce, and inherently unknowable. Our only epistemic access to the absolute properties of things is through inferential triangulation from their modus operandi—from the processes through which these manifest themselves.

In sum, processes without substantial entities are perfectly feasible in the conceptual order of things, but substances without processes are effectively inconceivable.

6. PROCESSES AND DISPOSITIONS

Processes stand coordinate to dispositions (though not necessarily substance-owned dispositions). On the one hand, processes are dispositionally structured modes of development:

Once started, any process involves a complex of characteristic dispositions for its own continuation and development. On the other hand, dispositions are processual—that is, are generally dispositions to activate or continue certain processes. The paradox of substance metaphysics arises through the infeasibility of specifying aprocessually exactly what a substance is—that is, in characterizing a substance without reference to process. Traditionally, substances are individuated by their properties, and there are supposed to be two sorts of properties:

• primary properties, which describe the substance as it is in and by itself
• secondary properties, which underlie the impact of substances upon others and the responses they invoke from them.

Now the difficulty is with saying what those primary properties of a substance—which, after all, are what is crucial to their existence—actually are, seeing that all we can ever determine is what sorts of reactions substances evoke elsewhere.

Things as traditionally conceived can no more dispense with dispositions than they can dispense with properties. Accordingly, a substance ontologist cannot get by without processes. If his things are totally inert—if they *do* nothing— they are pointless. Without processes there is no access to dispositions, and without dispositional properties, substances lie outside our cognitive reach. One can only observe what things *do*, via their discernible effects; what they *are*, over and above this, is something that always involves the element of conjectural imputation. And here process ontology takes a straightforward line: In its sight, things simply *are* what they *do*—or rather, what they dispositionally can do and normally would do.

The fact is that all we can ever detect about "things" relates to how they act upon and interact with one another—a substance has no *discernible*, and thus no justifiably attributable, properties save those that represent responses elicited from it in interaction with others. And so a substance metaphysics of the traditional sort paints itself into the embarrassing corner of having to treat substances as bare (propertyless) particulars because there is no nonspeculative way to say what concrete properties a substance ever has in and of itself. But a process metaphysics is spared this embarrassment because processes are, by their very nature, interrelated and interactive. A process—unlike a substance—can simply be what it does. And the idea of process enters into our experience directly and as such.

What renders the idea of process preeminently accessible to us is the processual nature of our own experience. And this is true (David Hume to the contrary notwithstanding) also, and indeed particularly, of the idea of *causal* process. As Whitehead observed:

> Our bodily experience is primarily an experience of the dependence of presentational immediacy upon causal efficacy. Hume's doctrine inverts this relationship by making causal efficacy, as an experience, dependence upon presentational immediacy. . . . It does not seem to be the sense of causal awareness that the lower living things lack, so much as variety of sense-presentation, and then vivid distinctness of presentational immediacy. . . . There is every indication of a vague feeling of causal relationship with the external world.[8]

Process philosophers thus cut the Gordian knot of Hume's critique of causality by insisting that we do indeed have the experience of causal efficacy—of the apprehensible power of things to produce observed results. Hume to the contrary notwithstanding, the causal efficacy of process is (often, at least) a matter of the feeling-character of our own experience and not a matter of a mysteriously mediated inference from constant conjunction.

Processes can conceivably make do without things. (As the example of "it is getting colder" shows, there can be unowned, "subjectless" processes which—unlike sneezing or dissolving—do not consist in the activities of things.) But no workable substance ontology can get on without a heavy reliance on processes, seeing that a process-detached thing is a fifth wheel. Substances can come upon the stage of consideration only through the mediation of processes. A process ontology thus greatly simplifies matters. Instead of a two-tier reality that combines *things* together with their inevitable coordinated *processes*, it settles for a one-tier ontology of process alone—at any rate, at the level of basics. For it sees things not just as the *products* of processes (as one cannot avoid doing) but also as the *manifestations* of processes—as complex bundles of coordinated processes. It replaces the troublesome ontological dualism of *thing* and *activity* with a monism of activities of different and differently organized sorts. If Ockham was right and simplicity is a crucial advantage in ontology, then process metaphysics clearly has much to offer.

3

Process and Particulars

SYNOPSIS

(1) Process philosophers do not deny things (substances). Rather, they reconceptualize them as manifolds of process. (2) Things are integrated and individuated as such by acting in a unitary way in the overall context at issue. Indeed, for process philosophers of an idealist cast of mind, things are individuated by being perceived as such, so that their unity is a unity of mental process. (3) P. F. Strawson's argument against processism, based on the supposed conceptual primacy of material bodies, is ultimately untenable. (4) The fact is that substance metaphysics has various serious problems of its own. (5) Processes themselves require no process-external unifiers. It is in the nature of the case that subsidiary processes combine to constitute complex, "supersidiary" processes. (6) Concrete (physical) particulars always arise through processes and operate in a processual setting. Indeed, involvement in a matrix of process is inherent in the very concept of a particular.

1. PARTICULARS

The mainstream philosophical tradition of the European West has been characterized by the dominance of a substance ontology that sees the world's particulars as being—typically and paradigmatically—material objects on the order of atoms or molecules or trees or planets. But, of course, the fact is that physical processes are every bit as qualified to count as concrete particulars as physical objects. This is clearly manifested by such items as rainstorms, heatwaves, famines, thunder-claps, rumors, and performances of a symphony. The world is obviously full of items—of "things," generally speaking—that it does not make sense to count as substances, as literally *sub-stantial things*: for example, discussions, songs, weather for-mations, headaches. Process ontologists go beyond this, however, in maintaining that the existence of particular indi-vidual things must, in the end, root in a unity of process—that such "things" as there are should always be understood in processual terms and perhaps even be somehow reduced to processes.

The problem of how substances (things with their coordi-nate properties and relations) can *act*—can destabilize their world so as to bring new states of affairs into being—has bedeviled substance philosophy from the outset. It engen-dered the paradoxes of Zeno. It underlay the critiques of Socrates, Plato, and Aristotle of their Pre-Socratic predeces-sors. It puzzled Descartes, Spinoza, and Leibniz; baffled Locke, Berkeley, and Hume. It impelled Kant to look beyond the empirically accessible world into a realm of things-in-themselves. It stirs amidst the great issues of traditional meta-physics: the problems of causation, of teleological purposiveness, of mind–body interaction. By sidestepping this problem through accepting processes as such from the outset—rather than trying to superimpose them on reluctant substances that afford them no natural hold—process meta-physics manages to avert a whole list of avoidable philosophi-cal difficulties.

Process philosophers do not, indeed, deny the reality of substances but merely reconceptualize them as manifolds of process. They are perfectly prepared to acknowledge substan-tial things, but see them rather in terms of processual activi-ties and stabilities. They hold that even where physical objects are concerned, the item is marked as the particular thing it is, not by a continuity of its material components or its physical form but by a processual or functional unity. (A sequential item-by-item replacement of parts need not necessarily trans-form one thing into another.) Heraclitus was only half right: We indeed do not step twice into the same *waters*, but we can certainly step twice into the same *river*. The unity of a particular that defines what it *is* consists in what it *does*. Process metaphysics accordingly stresses the need to regard physical things—material objects—as being no more than stability-waves in a sea of process.

Process philosophy owes much to John Locke's critique of substances. Good empiricist that he was, Locke insisted that we have no experiential contact with substances as such; we experience only their (putative) *effects*. Substances themselves are *something, we know not what;* it is only their causal impetus that we can ever come to experiential grips with. Accordingly, he held that it is in their *powers*—in the effect that they produce in us and in one another—that the being and nature of so-called substances will reside:

> *Powers* therefore justly make a great part of our complex ideas of substances. He that will examine his complex idea of gold, will find several of its ideas that make it up to be only powers; as the power of being melted, but of not spending itself in the fire; of being dissolved in *aqua regia*, are ideas as necessary to make up our complex idea of gold, as its color and weight: which if duly considered, are also nothing but different powers.[1]

Here proper philosophy joins in and simply takes the next logical step. Instead of seeing things (substances) as the *bearers* of powers, it sees them as *bundles* of powers.

Accordingly, process philosophy sees "things" as processual complexes possessing a functional unity instead of as substances individuated by a qualitative nature of some sort. On such a view, physical particulars become concrete instantiations of processual structures. As process philosophers see it, processuality can reflect the open-endedness of the world's physical and psychical continuities. The identity of things is discrete (digital); that of processes is continuous (analogic). *Things* are what they are, each standing apart in discrete separation from the rest in its individual identity. Only processes have an identity that is open ended and flowing, with one item capable of sliding into another.

An important merit of process philosophy is its ability to avert difficulties that afflict substantialism. Consider just one example. Seeing that future things do not (yet) exist, substance metaphysicians have difficulties with the future and cannot confidently accommodate it in their ontology. Process metaphysics avoids this difficulty from the outset. For the processual nature of the real means that the present constitution of things always projects beyond itself into one as yet unrealized future. You cannot claim that the arrow is moving now without committing yourself to its occupying a different position in the future. The future has its place within the processual present, seeing that the present is pregnant with the future (to use Leibniz's metaphor).

2. COMPLEXIFICATION

Processes are Janus faced: They look in two directions at once, inwards and outwards. They form part of wider (outer) structures but themselves have an inner structure of some characteristic sort. For processes generally consist of processes: microprocesses that combine to form macroprocesses. Process theorists often use organismic analogies to indicate this idea of different levels of units: Smaller, subordinate (or subsidiary) processes unite to form larger, superordinate (or supersidiary) process-units, as in cells combining into organs that, in turn, constitute organisms. For some processists this is a mere explanatory analogy; for others it is a paradigmatic model revelatory of the deep nature of things. But either way, the idea of a hierarchic assemblage of micro- into macro-units is a pervasive and characteristic aspect of process philosophy.

Processes, after all, come in all sizes, from the submicroscopic to the cosmic. And when smaller processes join to form large ones, the relation is not simply one of part to whole but of productive contributory to aggregate result. The notes are not just constituent parts of the song, they are the active elements of its production. The fact that the unity of process is itself processual is enormously convenient for process philosophy, because it means that not separate instrumentality of integration—process apart—is required to effect the information of processes.

Processual particulars are themselves clusters of processes. Like an organism, which is a cluster of integrated process (for nourishment, reproduction, etc.), process particulars are systemic wholes comprised of subordinate processes (in ways that factor "all the way down" in such processists as Leibniz and Boscovich). It was for good reason that Whitehead characterizes his processual metaphysics as a philosophy of organism. For processists, organisms are, if not the only natural particulars, then, at any rate, paradigmatic instances. As Hegel already indicated, an organism is "a microcosm, the center of Nature which has achieved an existence for itself in which the whole of inorganic Nature is recapitulated and idealized."[2]

Not only do processes come connected, but so do their aspects. Even as in ordinary experience a person immediately focuses on only some aspects of a larger complex whole, so in science we focus only on some features of the coherence we study and leave the others aside by an act of abstraction. Nature's processes stand connected with one another as integrated wholes—it is we who, for our own convenience, separate them into physical, chemical, biological, and psychological aspects.

Whitehead makes much of a category he terms *nexus* which is designed to provide for the combination and integration of his atomic process-units. A nexus represents "a particular fact of togetherness among actual entities,"[3] and reflects the fact that such entities make up organized groups or societies. But, in a way, this is a needless complication, forced on Whitehead by his commitment to process atomism of ultimately undissolvable processual units. Once this atomistic doctrine is abandoned, the matter becomes simplicity itself. Nothing is more natural than that microprocesses should join and combine into macroprocesses, and a process metaphysics that does not commit itself to a Whiteheadian atomism needs no special machinery to accommodate this fact, because it sees reality as processual "all the way down." A more satisfactory approach is that reflected in the doctrine of "synechism," introduced under this name by C. S. Peirce, who defined it as "that tendency of philosophical thought which insists upon the idea of continuity as of prime importance in philosophy,"[4] with particular stress on the idea that "a true continuum is something whose possibilities of determination no multitude of individuals can exhaust."[5] In the end, individuality can be conceived of in terms of unity of process which itself exhibits an unendingly deepening inner complexity.

3. ONGOING IDENTITY AS A MATTER OF ONGOING REIDENTIFIABILITY: AN IDEALISTIC PERSPECTIVE

As regards processes themselves, their identification has two aspects: combining an abstract character answering to a process-description ("a heat wave") with a concrete emplacement in a relational field connecting process-instantiations with one another (most conveniently by way of spatiotemporal positioning, as per "the heat wave that afflicted Atlanta last August"). Process identification thus involves two components: type specification and coordinative spatio-temporal placement.

Process philosophy accordingly holds that, given our own positioning within such a framework, individuation always involves some element of confrontation, of actual presentness of causal interaction. Identity rests on identifiability, and identification is something interactional—that is, it involves being identifiable as a single unit by an interagent. And such identification is always and unavoidably processual. Just this is grist to the processist mill, since what it shows is not, to be sure, that the existence of things as such involves process ontologically but rather that the identity of things involves processes conceptually.[6]

That processes are fundamental relative to things in the conceptual order of understanding emerges when we ask, Just what are those "properties" of things that are supposed to identify and individuate them? Clearly they are nothing other than the *effects* produced by those putative things upon ourselves and/or upon one another. But if this is so—if the very being and identity of things as the particulars they are consists in their status in a matrix of interaction—then the very nature of those identity-engendering factors (cause and effect, activity and passivity, action and interaction) make manifest the fundamentally processual nature of the "things" at issue.

Yet can one really identify particular instances of process without mentioning substances? Do not such processes as "the death of Nelson" or "the sacking of Constantinople" wear their linkage to things (substances) on their sleeves by virtue of the proper name involved? Of course they do! But not in a way that establishes the point supposedly at issue. For one can cash such substance-mention either *ostensively* by speaking of "*this* death" or "*that* sacking" or in terms of coordinate positives, eliminating that substance-mention processually, speaking of "the death (or sacking) occurring in coordination with such-and-such other occurrences." Accordingly, processes can be identified without bringing substantial things into it.

To be sure, many processists go further than such identification-fundamentality in holding that things are (or "are reducible to") process. The issue of their activity now steps into the foreground. With Leibniz, they see substances as centers of force of activity, and they consider what a substance *is* to reside in what that substance *does*. An adequate substance metaphysics cannot make do without processes. And at this point one is well en route to joining the process philosopher by acknowledging that the integrity of *things* consists in a unity of *process*—that things are being integrated and consolidated as such by acting in a unitary way in relation to others. Unity is as unity does: The unity of things is a unity of process. Processes are sufficient unto themselves and go along "doing their own thing." But substances are not; to be a substance is to *act* as a substance. It thus seems plausible to see existence in process-coordinated terms by taking existing to be a mode of activity. From this angle, existing is an *actus essendi*, a matter of "putting in an appearance," of something's projecting itself into reality by way of taking up a position on the world's stage. It is feasible to separate process from substances but effectively impossible to reverse the situation.

As these deliberations indicate, process ontology comes in two major forms or versions, the one stronger and causal (ontological), the other weaker and explanatory (conceptual):

- *Causal processism*: processes are causally/existentially fundamental relative to things; substances are merely appearances, the correlates of processes of "being taken to be a thing."
- *Conceptual processism*: processes are conceptually fundamental vis à vis things in that (1) the explanatory characterizations of what a thing is always involves recourse to a processual account of what that thing does; and (2) the identification of any particular thing as such always involves reference to various processes, a thing being constituted as what it is by means of identificating processes.

A variety of doctrines is accordingly at issue here, some of which take a distinctly more radical approach than others.

Process philosophers are not in general—and certainly need not be—immaterialists of the extreme, Berkeleyan sort. But they are in general idealists of one sort or another, for while mind is unlikely to be essential to the *existence* of material substances as such, it is certainly essential to its identification, explanation, classification, and the like—all of which are mental processes. If, indeed, there is no entity without identity, if to be a particular thing is to be identified as such, then even material particulars are *conceptually* (albeit not *causally*) dependent on the actual or potential operation of mental processes.

The salient point is that process philosophers tend to be realist about processes but idealist about substances. As they see it, there really are processes with a unity, identity, and structure of their own, independent of us. And at least some such processes are apprehensible by us through direct encounter in immediate experience. (And even if this is taken as a paradigm, we here have an at most *conceptual* idealism.) But substance, as process philosophers see it, is mere theory constructs. Substances do not present themselves in experience *as such* but only via their processual impacts. And since a substance is what it does and can do, the element of theoretical generalization is always involved. Accordingly, process philosophers incline to an idealistic view of substantial things.

Process philosophy's realism of trees construes "there actually are trees in the real world" idealistically as a somewhat oversimplified formulation (or abbreviation) for something that would—more fully and correctly formulated—run as follows:

> There occur (and so "exist") processes in "the real world"— processes which themselves nowise depend on the existence of minds and of which we humans can obtain a rough and imperfect (albeit ever more adequate) view via natural science. And in appropriate circumstances these processes nondelusionally engender the "here is a tree" response in duly prepared minds.

What is in view here are two sorts of "there is a tree" responses in our experience: (1) those that are delusional (misimpressions, optical illusions, posthypnotic responses to telegraph poles, etc.) and (2) those that are veridical—that occur when we "are really confronted by a tree," one that we see, touch, cut down, and so forth. And both are—obviously— determined via process of a certain sort.

And some process philosophers move even further in an idealistic direction. They hold, with Whitehead (and Hartshorne after him), that concrete things are not just experientiable but also somehow experiencing items. (Whitehead rejects materialism as an indulgence in "vacuous existence.") Whitehead's Reformed Subjectivist Principle, framed in opposition to Descartes's dualism, makes experiencing/experienced and subjective/objective indicative of different phases or aspects of everything that exists rather than classifications of ontologically distinct groups of entities. After all, things can be brought into the framework of experience not only as *experiencing* but also as *experienced*; they can be not only subjects of experience for themselves but also objects of experience for others. And so units of existence generally achieve their identity and individuality through the modus operandi of their processual interactions with others, their unity lying not so much in the mind as in the experience of their "beholders" (i.e., interagents). Their processual identity can, in the end, be of the "for another" sort.

However, to join the process metaphysician who sees particular things and their properties in terms of the "for another" relationship—that is, in terms of responses evoked in something or someone—is not necessarily to insist that this evocation proceeds by way of a *conscious* response. The gust of wind that sends the leaf aloft or the stone that breaks the window pane are—as interagents relative to that leaf or that pane—things (substances) of some sort. But, of course, they are not *consciously* perceived as such.

Leibniz—and Charles Hartshorne after him—see individuality and consciousness as essential to individuality—only what is *taken* as a unit by a thinking being actually qualifies as such. Yet this approach has its problems. It seems far too restrictive. It would surely be more plausible to take the line that whatever functions as a unit in interactions with others—whether responded to consciously or otherwise—qualifies as a particular. The potentialistic aspect is crucial here. It is not (as with Berkeley) that to be is to be *perceived* (to be a tree is to be perceived as such) but rather that to be a tree is to be *perceivable* as such. But, of course, perception is a mind-involving process and so *conceptually* (from the hermeneutic and explanatory standpoint) we have here a reference both to minds (idealism) and to their performances (processism). (To reemphasize: A conceptual processism is more plausible and more straightforwardly motivated than an ontological one.)

4. AGAINST STRAWSON'S CRITIQUE OF PROCESSISM

P. F. Strawson has argued in his influential book on metaphysics[8] that processism in all its versions is doomed to failure because physical objects—and, in particular, material bodies—are requisites for the idea of identifiable particulars in a way that is virtually indispensable to any viable metaphysical position. Strawson maintains that the identification of particulars in communication between speakers and hearers ("referential identification," as he terms it) necessarily requires reference to things possessed of material bodies, so that "we find that material bodies play a unique and fundamental role in particular identification" (56). As he sees it, processes will not do as basis for particular identification, because "if one had to give the spatial dimensions of such a process, say, [as] a death or a battle, one could only have the outline of the dying man or indicate the extent of the ground the battle was fought over" (57). Strawson accordingly holds that material bodies are a necessary precondition for any setting in which objective knowledge of particulars is to be possible.

In brief outline, Strawson's argument runs essentially as follows:

1. For objective and identifiable particulars to be knowable, some items must be (1) distinguishable from other coexistents and (2) reidentifiable over time.
2. These conditions (viz., distinguishability and reidentifiability) can be met only by material objects (i.e., particulars with material bodies).

If this line of reasoning is indeed correct, then processism is untenable in metaphysics. For it is perfectly clear that any viable metaphysic must have room for identifiable particulars, and if these are to be had only on the basis of a material-object substantialism, then process metaphysics is a lost cause.

This argumentation, however, has its problems. To begin with, Strawson would have been well advised to add yet a third item: that individuals must be not only distinguishable and reidentifiable by a *particular* knower but interpersonally and intersubjectively distinguishable and reidentifiable throughout a *community* of knowers. Yet even with premiss 1 strengthened in this way, premiss 2 does not hold water.

Strawson maintained that:

> The only objects which can constitute [the space-time framework essential to interpersonal communication] are those which confer upon it their own fundamental characteristics. That is to say they must be three dimensional objects with some endurance through time. . . . They must collectively have enough diversity, richness, stability, and endurance to make possible just that conception of a single unitary [space-time] framework which we possess.[9]

The process philosopher will have no quarrel with any of this. However, Strawson then proceeded straightaway to draw a deeply problematic conclusion:

> Of the categories of object which we recognize, only those satisfy these requirements which are, or possess, material bodies—in the broad sense of the expression. Hence given a certain general feature of the [space-time committed] conceptual scheme which we possess, and given the character of available major categories, things which are, or possess, material bodies must be [epistemologically] basic particulars.[10]

To its decisive detriment, Strawson's argument simply begs the question here. For all of the features that his analysis require (spatiotemporal stability and endurance, diversity, richness, interpersonal accountability, and the like) are possessed every bit as much by *physical processes* as by the things that "are or possess *material bodies*." It is not material substances (things) alone that can be distinguished and reidentified within nature's spatiotemporal framework but occurence-complexes (processes) as well. Processes are physically realized without being literally embodied. And the one is no less confrontable and capable of ostensive indication than the other ("that lion," "that tornado"). Strawson sees substances as conceptually prior to process because he takes those processes to be paradigmatic which reflects the doings of substances (like births of animals or blossomings of flowers). The sorts of physical processes which—like cold front movements or lightning flashes—are nowise tied to identified physical particulars do not figure in his scheme of things. Only by an act of deeply problematic fiat is Strawson able—even within the restricted confines of his own analysis—to advantage and priortize material bodies over physical processes. Strawson's insistence that epistemically basic particulars must be identifiable by ostension holds every bit as much for instances of physical process as for particular material bodies. (Indeed, as we shall see, it is theoretically possible to reconceptualize material bodies as complexes of physical processes, while the reverse—the general reconceptualization of physical processes as complexes of material objects—is just not on.) Strawson's reasoning sets out from the quite appropriate Kantian observation that objective distinguishability and reidentifiability require the machinery of a spatiotemporal matrix. The objectification of experience calls for a general, all-encompassing framework of coordination, viz. the sphere-time framework. But at this point his reasoning goes astray. For, as he sees it, a spatiotemporal framework demands—and can only be determined in terms of—ordering relations among material objects. But there are, in fact, other physically "embodied" items distinct from material bodies that can serve this function equally well—to wit, processes. For as long as processes have both position and duration—as long as like a flame (rather than a sound) or a wedding ceremony (rather than something more ethical like a divorcement)—there are items that have a sufficiently definite place and a sufficiently long lifespan to serve as coordinate markers. Processes too, in sum, can serve to define and constitute the required spatio-temporal framework.

Strawson's position is plausible only because he accepts the question-begging Process Reducibility Thesis that insists on seeing all processes in terms of the activities of things (substances). From this standpoint, all processes are owned and we are to look at them from a specifically genitive point of view: the death of Caesar, or the great clash of the armies of Napoleon and Tsar Alexander I at Borodino. But this of-indicated object-correlativity (of that person, of these two armies) takes too narrow a view of the matter. It reflects only the particular (i.e., owned) modality of processes at issue and not their processuality as such. Where processes are more broadly conceived, their object-correlativity can disappear from view.

The point is that while we can indication-identify various concrete processes genitively—as per "this birth" = "the birth of Julius Ceasar"—proceeding in terms of process-type plus substance-correlative possession, we can no less easily in dualism identify them positionally in terms of process-type plus location: "this birth" = "the birth at such-and-such a spatio-temporal location." And, of course, the referential markers that orient us in space-time need not be substantial ("the town center of Greenwich") but can be processual ("the pole" = "the place where the compass needle spins around evenly").

Accordingly, Strawson's argumentation misses its target. It is simply not the case that material objects are the indispensable basis for a framework of knowable particulars. Physical processes of a suitable sort can accomplish this essential task equally well.

But the irony here is that Strawson's basic standard of priority (viz. "referential identification") is itself altogether processual.

5. Difficulties of Substantialism

Then, too, there is the fact that substance ontology has serious difficulties of it own.

One major problem with a traditionalist ontology of substances and properties lies in the difficulty of handling change-indicative processes and activities on this basis. One can, without difficulty, accommodate conjunctions: "In 1900 John was born, and in 1920 John was a young man." But the idea of a *process*—of development and maturation as inherent in the idea of John's being a young man in 1920 *because* he was born in 1900 and grew older in the ordinary way—cannot be represented in these simply conjunctive terms.

Some process philosophers take a still more decidedly negative view of substance metaphysics, however. For example, Johanna Seibt has argued[11] that the idea of a substantial object as standardly conceived in the philosophical literature is logically incoherent. A somewhat simplified version of her argument runs as follows: Substances as standardly conceived are regarded as objects that persist over time and continue as self-identical despite changes of properties in the course of time's passage. On this basis, substance philosophies have generally committed themselves to three principles:

I. *The principle of transtemporal identity.* A substance (individual, object) is a persistent that continues to be identical with itself throughout its career:

$(\forall\ u)\ (\forall\ v)\ (\forall\ x)\ ([u = x\text{-at-}t\ \&\ v = x\text{-at-}t'] \rightarrow u = v)$

II. *Leibniz's Law.* Substances are numerically identical if they are qualitatively identical, that is, if (and only if) they have all of their properties in common:

$$(\forall \ x) \ (\forall \ y) \ (x = y \leftrightarrow (\forall \ F) \ [Fx \leftrightarrow Fy] \ )$$

III. *The principle of temporal change.* Substances are bound to change some of their properties over time:

$$(\forall \ x) \ ([t \neq t'] \rightarrow (\exists \ F) \ [T_t \ (Fx) \ \& \sim T_{t'}(Fx)])$$

The following course of reasoning establishes the systemic incoherence (collective incompatibility) of these three principles:

1. $t \neq t'$ by assumption
2. For any individual x there will be a property F such that:
    $T_t \ (Fx) \ \& \sim T_{t'} \ (Fx)$ from 1, III
3. $T_t \ (Fx) \ \& \ T_{t'} \ ([not\text{-}F]x)$ from 2
4. $F(x\text{-}at\text{-}t) \ \& \ not\text{-}F(x\text{-}at\text{-}t')$ from 3
5. $x\text{-}at\text{-}t \neq x\text{-}at\text{-}t'$ from 4, II
6. $x\text{-}at\text{-}t = x\text{-}at\text{-}t'$ from I
7. theses 5 and 6 are mutually inconsistent

The conjoint acceptance of I–III accordingly leads ad absurdum. The principles governing the conceptualization of substances that have been standard among substance ontologists are involved in an incoherence.

To be sure, there are various ways of addressing this apory. A conflict among propositions can always be resolved in different ways by replacing some of them through introducing the necessary distinctions.[12] But no matter how one turns here, the fact remains that the standard and orthodox approach to substance metaphysics cannot be maintained as is—that it must be subjected to complexifications and sophistications that undermine its appeal as the "natural and straightforward" approach that it purports to be.

6. The Origination of Particulars

How do particulars originate and terminate in time? A process philosophy unable to come to satisfactory terms with this issue would ipso facto be in serious difficulty. In this context, however, one category of processes requires special consideration, namely those which, like starting/stopping and birth/death and beginning/ending, are oriented toward the anterior or posterior nonexistence of the item at issue. To be sure, subsuming these eventuations under the characterization of a process requires a recourse to such unorthodox transitions as those between existence and nonexistence (or the reverse), and thus means that we must take the somewhat unorthodox step of treating *nonexistence* as a (sort of) state of affairs.

Classical substance metaphysics considers substance origination to be instantaneous: there is a "moment of conception," an instant of origination, prior to which the substance never existed and after which the substance as such always exists up to some subsequent time of its expiry. It is clear, however, that such instantaneous origination is not the only theoretically available possibility. An alternative view would contemplate the prospect of an *interval* of concrescence—a noninstantaneous coming (rather than springing) into existence akin to the building of a house or a ship. (At just what temporal instant or point did the *Queen Mary* come into existence?) This alternative model accordingly sees origination itself as a process, envisioning a gestation period between nonexistence and existence—an interval during which the thing at issue comes into being, that is, literally emerges into existence. Such a contrasting way of looking at the matter of origination in terms of transitional processuality characterizes the position of most process philosophers. Process metaphysicians—preeminently Whitehead—insist that concrete (physical) particulars always arise through processes and inevitably owe them their very existence. And, indeed, its involvement and enmeshment in a matrix of process is inherent in the very concept of a particular.

And if coming-into-being is itself actually to be a process, then there has to be a period or interval of transition—of reification or concrescence—during which it can neither be said truly that the thing at issue actually exists nor on the other hand that it does not exist at all.[13]

Three salient facts must be noted about such an interval of substance-origination:

1. It is a "fuzzy" interval that has no definite, clearly specifiable temporal beginning or end.
2. During this interval we can say neither that the thing (already) exists nor that it does not (yet) exist; during that gestation period the substance's existence is actually indeterminate.
3. If the world had been annihilated during this interval, then it would neither be correct to say that the thing has (ever) existed in the world nor that it has not (ever) existed. The theses that the thing has existed (at some time or other) would also have to be classified as indeterminate. (From an ontological point of view, it could be said that, figuratively speaking, the world "has not managed to make up its mind" about the existence of the thing. The world itself is, in this regard, indeterminate.)

As these observations indicate, a conceptually rigorous implementation of the idea of reification as a process—of a thing's coming into existence over a course of time—will require the deployment of two historically unorthodox items of concept-machinery:

i. a "fuzzy logic"—or at any rate a fuzzy mathematics—that puts the conception of indefinite (imprecisely bounded) intervals and regions at our disposal[14]
ii. a semantics of truth-value gaps, serving to countenance propositions that are neither (definitely) true nor (definitely) false but indeterminate in lacking a classical truth value.[15]

Neither of these unorthodoxies is in any way absurd, and both represent theoretical resources that are today well known and widely employed in logic and the theory of information management. (Indeed, the second idea goes back all the way to Aristotle himself, in the sea battle example of the discussion of future contingency in chapter 9 of *De interpretatione*.[16])

4

Process and Universals

SYNOPSIS

(1) One of the perennial key issues of metaphysics is the "problem of universals"—of how to account for the nature and status of types, kinds, and similar modes of generality. A process approach to universals affords a natural and economic way of addressing this problem. (2) Creativity— the initiation of novelty—is a salient feature of a process-laden world, and process philosophy sees this as a pivotal feature of the real. However, the world's processes bring not just new individuals (new items) into being but new universals (new kinds) as well. (3) Taxonomic complexification—the emergence of new modes of existence time—is accordingly one of the characteristic doctrines of process philosophy.

1. PROCESS AND "THE PROBLEM OF UNIVERSALS"

Let us now turn from particulars to universals. Here too process philosophy has merit. For the machinery of process metaphysics also provides a helpful resource for dealing with the classical philosophical problem of the nature and status of universals—those "types" and "kinds" and similar modes of generality.

The universals of traditional metaphysics are principally of two sorts: (1) *perceptual universals* (colors, odors, felt textures), which relate to the impact of things on the conscious percipients, and (2) *natural kinds* which arise through the patterns of interaction-impact that things make on one another. And it is important not to conflate the two so as to arrive at an extreme idealism that exaggerates the role of mind in the world's course of things and sees all speciation as mind-imposed. But what, then, of the status of such universals?

Classically, there are three rival theories of "universals"—theories which see them, respectively, as:

- *made by minds operating on their own* (nominalism or conventionalism): Universals are purely mental artifacts that are imputed to things by minds in virtue of their (the mind's) own operations.
- *found (by minds) in things* (realism): Universals are mind-independent preexisting aspects of things that are—or can be—perceived by minds as independently existing features of the objects they deal with.
- *generated in mind–world interaction* (conceptualism): Universals arise out of the cognitive interaction between minds and things (and thus are neither purely mental artifacts nor mind-independent factors).

Nominalism sees universals as made by minds alone; realism would have them lie in the mind-independent nature of things alone; conceptualism takes them to arise in a processual interaction of minds with things. Realism has two main forms, a platonic realism that sees universals as self-subsistent, and a causal realism that sees them as inhering in the mode of interaction that things have with one another.

From the angle of process philosophy, however, a significant point is that each of these several traditional theories of universals sees them as rooted in processes of some sort (whether mental or physical). And so the mechanisms of process philosophy will, in any event, provide a natural and virtually unavoidable instrument for addressing this key metaphysical issue. From process philosophy's point of view, the pivotal fact is that all of the classical theories of universals take them to be products engendered by processes of some sort. Even a platonic realism which sees the universals themselves (the ideas) as subsisting in a changeless, world-detached realm of their own is able to connect these abstractions to the things of this world only by inventing a process of some sort (to wit, Plato's "participation").[1]

But while any viable theory of universals points toward a process approach, process philosophy as such is not neutral about those different views of universals. Insofar as it sees process as ontologically fundamental, it does accept that (at least some) processes have a unity, structure, and identity not dependent wholly and exclusively on the mind's operations. A full-blooded process metaphysics accordingly rejects, at any rate, one of those classical theories of universals as far as process-types themselves are concerned, namely, a pure nominalism or conventionalism.

But why should one adopt the process point of view toward universals? What is it that links the various instances of a kind and makes those different items into so many instantiations of that "one selfsame kind"? What do various material objects (grains of sand, say, and goldfish) have in common? What do all those different ways of writing and printing the letter A all share with one another? As the process philosopher sees it, what is at bottom at issue here is a matter of lawful modus operandi rather than of common properties of some sort. Those different scribbles are made into letters because of their lawful functioning in communicative contexts. Kinds are constituted as such not because their instances exhibit a commonality in which they *are* but because they exhibit a commonality in what they *do*. Those very different material objects are made into instances of this particular type-kind through their functioning under the aegis of laws of physics, of chemistry, and so forth. Process lies at the bottom of it where universals are concerned.

At the basis of the relevant deliberations lies the fact that processes can, do, and must have a structure of patterns and periodicities that render them in-principle repeatable. And to say that an item has a *structure* of some sort is to attribute to it a feature that other items can in principle also have.[2] But, of course, structure, though repeatable and abstractable, is itself not a mere abstraction; in its very nature it is a feature that a concrete item concretely exhibits. Abstraction does not *create* structure but presupposes it. In Hegelian terminology, a particular process represents a *concrete* universal—it not only *instantiates* its processual structure but *has* it. There is no reason why that which instances a property-type must of necessity be a thing. Property instantiations can in theory be free floating and thing-detached—like the bright spots one sees in one's visual field after pressing one's eye with a finger. But a concrete instantiation of a process-type will always itself have to be a process.

For the substance metaphysician, a universal is a second-order property, a higher-level feature that various thing-properties have in common and that link them into one single type. Thus, the universal *redness* is what is common and shared by this apple's redness, your sunset's redness, that rose's redness, and so on. For the process metaphysician, by contrast, all the processes of a given type constitute a field or realm; even as all economic processes constitute the economic realm and all biological processes constitute the biological realm, all physical processes constitute the physical realm. And from the angle of a process metaphysics, the conceptually advantageous fact is that realms are composed of their subdomains by way of straightforward inclusion—and thus in a way in which property-universals are not and cannot be composed of the properties that *constitute them.* Realms are *megaprocesses*, as it were. And such megaprocesses need not necessarily be continuous in space and time; it makes perfect sense to see all processes of the same sort (all pencil sharpenings, for example) as constituting not merely a processual thing-kind but also as thereby constituting a spatiotemporally distributed megaprocess.

In particular, colors, say, or numbers or poems lend themselves naturally to a processual account. Take phenomenal colors, for example. A mental process such as perceiving or imagining a certain shade of red is simply a way of perceiving redly or imagining redly—that is to say, in a certain particular way. And here, the relevant universal is not the abstract quality *red*, but the generic process at issue in perceiving (seeing, apprehending) something *redly*. (Qualities of this sort are fundamentally adverbial rather than adjectival in nature.) That purported universal—the shade of phenomenal red—

ceases to be a mysterious *object* of some sort and is now construed as a shared, specifiable feature of familiar large-scale processes (perceivings, imaginings) that provides their integrating linkage.

How distinct minds can conceive the same universal is now no more mysterious than how distinct birds can share the same song. In both cases it is simply a matter of doing things in the same generic way. Otherwise mysterious-seeming universals such as odors or fears are simply shared structural features of mental processes. The "universal" unity of a quality inheres in the unity of the reactive process at issue. (For the process philosopher, quality, too, is what quality does.) Again, physical (rather than perceptual) universals (being an acid, say, or being a conductor of electricity) root in the interactive processes of things. They, too, are defined by the features characteristic of the processes at issue. Such universals are inherently processual: They are what they are by virtue of what they do. On this basis, universals can be conceptualized as structural features of processes, and thereby they pose no particular difficulties for the process metaphysician.

To be sure, someone might object:

> Those process philosophers are caught up in a confusion. The recital of a poem on the performance of an opera are indeed processes, but the poem and the opera themselves are not. And analogously, the living of the life history of a person is process, but the person is not.

But this objection is readily met. The opera and the poem themselves are clearly nothing but recipes for performing those processes (of productions, readings, recitals, and performances)—they are, if you will, programs for instantiating (and thus, by inversion, also for reidentifying) these processes. And analogously, a person is nothing other than the (in this case) unique instantiating instance of that particular life history. Thus, the "thing" at issue is simply the collectivity processes that actualize and embody "it" as the processual item it indeed is.

Processes, seen abstractly, are inherently structural and programmatic—and, in consequence, universal and repeatable. To be a process is to be a process of a certain structural sort, a certain specifiable make-up. What concretizes processes of a given abstract characterization—a rain shower, for example—is simply their spatiotemporal emplacement within the wider matrix of natural process, their positioning by way of concrete realizations or instantiations in the framework of reality. And so a particular instance of a process is, by its very nature, a concrete universal—any actually occurrent process is *at once* concrete (context-specific) and universal (type-instantiating). And there is, presumably, little or no problem about process types, because these can be accounted for in terms of a commonality of programmatic structure. Since something cannot be a process without exhibiting structure, it must be of a process-type. With processes, universality is inescapable.

And so, on the process approach, universals are pulled down from the Platonic realm to become structural features of the ways in which the world's processes transpire. Recourse to a process approach is once again a useful problem-solving device through achieving economy by cutting through various layers of needless ontological complication.

2. NOVELTY, INNOVATION, CREATIVITY

Given its commitment to the centrality of time, process philosophy considers the specious present to be the movable entryway separating a settled and determinate past from an open and (as yet) unrealized and indeterminate future. And since this future always brings new situations to realization, the present is ever the locus of novelty, innovation, and creativity.

A preprogrammed world of the sort derogated by William James as a "block universe" is anathema to processists. Like him, they react sharply against a predeterminist position where everything is constrained to be by what has been and any replay of events would lead to the same preprogrammed result that precludes not only choice and chance but grants the dead hand of the past an absolute authority over the future. Such innovation-precluding preprogramming is wholly at odds with the creative openness in nature and in human affairs upon which process philosophers have always insisted. A Nietzschean world of eternal recurrence is anathema to processists. As they see it, processual novelty sets limits on the extent to which a particular domain—be it nature at large or human affairs—falls subject to the automatism of mechanized routines. They insist upon maintaining the creative impetus of natural process which abrogates what Whitehead somewhere called "the tedium of indefinite repetition" that leaves no room for novelty and rigidly circumscribes the world's processual nature.

Stephen C. Pepper was a process philosopher who devoted much attention to clarifying the idea of novelty. As Pepper has it, novelty is a pervasive quality of the real. He distinguished three senses of the concept. First, there is the novelty of uniqueness. Every event differs from every other event merely by its occurrence; each is unique and hence novel simply by being this-here-now and no other. Second, we have the intrinsic vividness of occurrences "there is first the fresh event intrinsically glowing with novelty."[3] Yet because the novelties of uniqueness and vibrancy grow stale, a third sort of novelty arises: intrusive novelty. It is manifest in the unexpected and the jarring; and in its extreme case, it is tantamount to destabilization and conflict. Hence the category of creativity, as the source of novelty in all its senses, brings to the world process special hazards, and must therefore be supplemented with another category—order. Cosmic process, for Pepper, proceeds through the dialectic of novelty and order.

Innovation by definition involves novelty, and very different things can be at issue here. Those of principal concern to process philosophy are

- *ontological* innovation: new things, processes, products, states of affairs (*Note:* "New" in the presently operative sense will mean new in kind)
- *phenomenical* innovation: new types of events or courses of events (natural or personal histories)
- *epistemic* (or conceptual or cognitive) innovation: new sorts of knowledge, ideas, information, problems, questions.

Perhaps no form of novelty is more intractable from the predictive point of view than conceptual novelty—innovations in ideas and conceptions. To predict a new sort of thing or event, we need not produce it; but to predict—conceivably and specifically—a new idea or conception, we must produce it at the time. By its nature epistemic innovation can only be predicted in abstracto and cannot be preindicated in its concrete detail.

After all, human creativity and inventiveness defies predictive foresight. We realize full well *that* there will be unforeseen innovations in art, literature, technology, science, business, and other large-scale areas of human endeavor in the decades and centuries ahead. But of course we cannot predict what they will be. We can predict *that* new modes of communication will still be invented by the year 3000 but not *what* they will be. (To characterize them now in detail would be to invent them now.) The fruits of human ingenuity always come as a surprise (and frequently an unwelcome one). If rational foresight could anticipate its operations, creativity as such would not exist. In particular, the course of discovery—of cognitive innovation—is a major source of predictive incapacity. The prediction of novelty is obviously infeasible in those instances where specifying the purported innovation at issue involves anticipating it. The historian can say that "X was the first person to state (or realize) that the human body consists principally of water" but no predictive sage can foretell in advance that "X will be the first person to state (or realize) that the human body consists principally of water." Not only would any such prediction be automatically self-falsifying, but the claim at issue is literally paradoxical.

The crucial fact here is that of impredictability. When we see an innovation—whatever it be—first emerging in nature's handwriting on the wall of existence, we cannot yet tell what is to come. Process philosophy does not deny the existence of patterns as such—quite on the contrary: It insists that processes themselves both instantiate and transmit structural patterns. What process metaphysics denies is the exclusive prevalence of inevitable preestablished patterns that make prediction unfailingly possible. It is against the background of an emphasis on the role of chance and choice in nature that the process philosopher's emphasis on novelty and innovation must be understood.

Kant and Laplace envisioned the astronomical development of new planetary objects. Darwinian evolution contemplated the emergence of new organic species. Peirce generalized biological evolution into a "cosmogenic philosophy." And Bergson stressed nature's creativity in the ongoing production of physical novelty, envisioning a pervasive vital impulse (*élan vital*) of creative evolution in nature which impels it to fill every ecological niche with endlessly variable forms of organic life. All of these thinkers saw creative process as a prominent and characteristic feature of nature's modus operandi. However, the crucial thing with innovation is the origination not just of new things or items but of new *kinds*—and thus of new processes. William James put the salient point as follows:

> Novelty, as empirically found, doesn't issue by jumps and jolts; it leaks in insensibly. . . . All the old identities at last give out, for the fatally continuous infiltration of otherness warps things out of every original rut.[4]

With any sort of evolution-oriented doctrine, processism included, the emergence of novel kinds—the origination of species—is a principal factor.

Clearly, genuine novelty does not arise simply through the mere existence of something new—it requires more: to wit, either the origination of a new *kind* of thing or else of a new *condition* of things on a larger basis. In principle, there are two sorts of novelty: novelty as to type and novelty as to item. Relative to a printing of a, this next a is new as to item but not type, while this b is additionally new as to type. But where processes are concerned, mere kind repetition is productive of novelty: A process of the kind pp (that is, a p-repetition) is itself a new and different kind of process. Even apparent repetitions of the same process are not all that repetitive. As the world runs, things are never quite the same the second time around. Even with what seem to be "mere repetitions," new patterns emerge and there is change (innovation) at the level of thing-types. The crucial thing about nature (or "reality"), from the process point of view, is that it constitutes the theater of operation of creative processes—processes that themselves engender new processes. Nature acts much as the expert chess player who configures moves into novel and innovative combinations and is able to produce an ever-widening array of new products (new phenomena) even from a finite and limited starting point.

The prominence of creative process is brought home to us in the inner impetus to create something new that is characteristic of the fine arts. They have been driven, in the West at least, by an ongoing urge to innovation, aimed not just at creating new objects but new forms, modes, genres, and styles. From the *ars nova* of the sixteenth century to the era of Schönberg and Cage—and beyond—the creators of music have ever projected a new beginning for the whole venture. The avant garde has been with us in every age. Repetition, uniformity, monotony are terms of derogation in art as elsewhere. And this situation is seen by process philosophers as emblematic of a universal phenomenon that affords an inspiration to their theory and a confirmation of its correctness.

3. TAXONOMIC COMPLEXIFICATION

The classical, Platonic view of universals is that they constitute a fixed and unchanging realm. Here, process metaphysics takes a very different line, adopting the ideas of C. S. Peirce. Peirce saw the opening up of new domains of phenomena in developmental terms. Early in world history, before the evolution of complex molecules, there was no place for biological laws; in the era of Neanderthal man there was no room for political economy. As the cosmos grows older, new modes of natural organization gradually evolve to afford new phenomena that are governed by emerging laws of their own—laws that previously had no opportunity to come into operation. There is progression from laws of individual physical particles to laws of increasingly elaborate organized complexes thereof. Since the universe affords a varied panorama of modalities of physical process evolving over time, a science that reflects this will continue to find new grist for its mill.

There are in principle two quite different sorts of complexity hierarchies. One kind is a hierarchy of material systems related by physical inclusion: particles, atoms, molecules, macrolevel physical objects, stars and planets, galaxies, galactic clashes, and so forth; or again, molecules, cells, organs, organisms, colonies, and the like. However, such *physical* hierarchies of compositional structure stand in contrast to *law* hierarchies of physical order with stages moving from base-level laws that govern phenomena to higher-level laws coordinating laws, and upward to laws coordinating laws that coordinate laws, and so on. The latter sort of hierarchy of lawful order does not presuppose the former. It can go on indefinitely even in a world whose structural-complexity depth is finite: Complexity of operation does not require complexity in point of physical constitution. Even a world that is finite in the structural complexity of its physical constitution may well exhibit a "hierarchy of nomic orders" with an ongoing sequence of levels of higher-order laws.

But one can go still further.

Even a system that is finitely complex both in its physical make-up and in its basic law structure might yet be infinitely complex in its actual *operations* over time. For the operations of a structurally finite and nomically finite system can yet exhibit an infinite intricacy in *operational or functional complexity*, manifesting this limitless diversity in the working out of its processes rather than at the spatiostructural or nomic level. Even were the number of constituents of nature to be small, the ways in which they can be combined to yield products in space-time might yet be infinite. Think here of the examples of letters/syllables/words/sentences/paragraphs/books/genres/ libraries/library systems. Even a finite nature can, like a typewriter with limited keyboard, yield a body of text that admits of potentially endless variation. It can produce a steady stream of new phenomena—"new" not necessarily in kind but in their functional interrelations and thus in their theoretical implications—on this basis of which our knowledge of nature's operations is continually enhanced and deepened.

There is no need to assume a "ceiling" to such a sequence of levels of integrative complexity of processual order.

The different levels of each exhibit an order of their own. The phenomena we attain at the nth level can have features whose investigation takes us to the $(n + 1)$th. New phenomena and new laws presumably arise at every level of integrative order. The different facts of nature can generate conceptually new strata of operation that yield a potentially unending sequence of levels, each giving rise to its own characteristic principles of organization, themselves quite unpredictable from the standpoint of the other levels. Even a world that is relatively simple as regards its basic operations can come to have an effectively infinite *cognitive* depth, once one proceeds to broaden one's notion of a natural phenomenon to include not just the processes themselves and the products they produce but also the *relationships* among them.

And there is no reason why this sort of thing cannot go on and on. For the system always exhibits new patterns of processual order over time, and so there is always more to be learned about it. There will always be new levels of functional complexity of operation to be investigated with such a system. It will always be possible to elaborate yet further levels of structured relationship.

From such a perspective, the role of processual innovation is a crucial factor of nature. And the result of such innovation is not just the organization of new *things* but the organization of new *kinds*—not just of individuals but of universals. The ongoing development of taxonomic complexity is a key feature of the world.

This matter of radical novelty is one of the pivotal and characteristic themes of process philosophy. Whitehead, for example, saw in creativity a "category of the ultimate"—it is a "universal of universals" that is at work in every department of nature, everywhere bringing novelty to realization.[5] For him, creativity represented the very essence of reality: To exist is to be creative, in the first instance of oneself (self-creation) and by reflection influencing the self-creation of the other existents to which things are linked by process of interaction. With Whitehead, as with Bergson, it is through the impetus of creativity that all of the processes that constitute nature transpire, with each day seeing the drawing of a new phase in the world's creative advance—the ongoing transit of world history into pioneer territory where nothing and no one has been before.

To be sure, it is certainly *possible* to minimize the significance of novelty by conceiving of the role of process in nature as consisting in a fixed number of elemental process types themselves fixed for all time—through whose combination and interplay all other natural processes arise. But such a hardedged, atomistically stabilitarian view of process does violence to the spirit of the enterprise of process philosophizing. Even as Darwin abolished the Aristotelian fixity of biological species, so process philosophy denies the unalterable fixity of the various species of natural kinds—and, indeed, of natural processes at large. It sees processes not as coming in hardedged inflexible types but as fluid and shifting, themselves in an ongoing course of processual development, with innovation and novelty—the fading of old types and the emergence of new ones—as ever being the order of the day. Processuality does not happen simply at the ground-floor level of things, events, and phenomena. The *types* of items at issue can change as well. Darwin's discovery holds not just in biology but everywhere: The fundamental novelty at issue with creativity and the innovation of new kinds of species is pervasive. Reclassification is a constant necessity, since species, too, are transitory and impermanent, with the old opening the way for development of the new. The theory of evolution powerfully encouraged the view of the universe as a processual manifold rather than as assemblage of fixed and unchanging essences that perdure unaltered over the course of time. Short of introducing a deus ex machina of some sort, there is no machinery-internal reason why novelty and innovation should ever come into a domain of things—as the difficulties encountered by substantialists from Epicurus to Newton attest. But with processes the situation is very different. For since processes are by nature transient and transformatory, they naturally make room for evolutionary development. After all, novelty emergence and innovation are themselves types of process.

Process metaphysicians thus see nature as a stage setting for a creativity that engenders radical novelty. Such creativity clearly requires room for the alternativeness of inde-termination. In general, the world's processes do not totally determine their successors and are not totally determined by the predecessors. Process theorists accordingly maintain that nature exhibits some modicum of a *causal slack* that makes room for chance and choice, for novelty, innovation, and cre-ativity. As they see it, nature's processes follow patterns—but not in a rigidly programmed and preordained predetermined way. The world constantly affords illustrations of pattern-breaking novelty and innovation. Accordingly, insistence on the "creative evolution" of new patterns, new modes of process—new universals, in short—is a characteristic doctrine of the school.

5

Process Philosophy of Nature

SYNOPSIS

(1) The basic idea of a process philosophy of nature is to view the world as a unified macroprocess consisting of a myriad of duly coordinated subordinate microprocesses. (2) Such an approach provides a straightforward means of accounting for the world's operations, and affords an efficient instrumentability for the scientific understanding of the real. (3) Nature's laws characterize the modus operandi of its processes, but these laws themselves are almost certainly processual and transitory, reflecting the varying modes of order prevalent among nature's changing and evolving processes. (4) Process philosophy sees space and time not as a constituting process-neutral framework within which natural processes transpire but rather as themselves an inherent feature of cosmic process at large—a manifold of order among such processes. (5) The process aspect of physical reality is manifest most clearly and strikingly at the quantum level. (6) The theory of evolution has been one of the main inspirations for process philosophy. It affords a clear model for how small-scale individual processes (on the order of individual lives) can productively combine to engender large-scale processes (on the order of the development of organic types). Its stress on innovation gives a decidedly optimistic cast to process philosophy, subject to the evolution-inspired idea of an ongoing development of forms that are not simply new but also "higher" in achieving greater levels of complexity and sophistication. (7) The process approach to

the philosophy of nature is validated vis-à-vis its alternatives through its smooth harmonization with our world-picture as natural science reveals it.

1. BASIC IDEAS OF A PROCESS PHILOSOPHY OF NATURE

We now turn to an examination of the characteristic features of a process philosophy of nature. The basic idea of the process is to view the world as a unified macroprocess that consists of a myriad of duly coordinated subordinate microprocesses. A clear contrast-case to such a view of the real is afforded by classical atomism based on the Democritean conception of atoms and the void. While the reciprocal relationship of such items—atoms and the void—is supposed to give rise to motion (and so to processes), these fundamental resources themselves are unprocessual items that stand entirely outside the order of process, seeing that, as classically conceived, they themselves are wholly impervious to change. On the other hand, a physics based exclusively on fields and forces that operate on their own, without any embedding in substantial things of some sort, is the quintessence of a process philosophy of nature. These items—fields and distributions of force—allow processual change to occur "all the way through," so to speak.

But what advantages does such a process-geared view have to offer? The answer ultimately lies in the extent to which it enables us to synthesize and understand the cognitive phenomena that confront us throughout the study of the natural world we inhabit.

In principle there is a substantial variety of different sorts of process—mental, symbolic, ritualistic, mathematical, and so forth. What distinguishes the *physical* processes at issue in natural science from the others is their emplacement in the coordinative order of space, time, and causality. Of course, every sort of process has its own rules—is "lawful" in some manner or other. But physical processes are characterized as such by the fact that their modus operandi admits of location within the space-time-causality framework provided for by the laws of nature. At every level of scale, from the subatomic microcosm to the cosmic macrocosm, we find a stirring of processes both characteristic and constitutive of the physical manifold at issue.

To be sure, processes that are not themselves strictly speaking physical can nevertheless be given a physical representation or embodiment. The symbolic process at issue in a musical composition is physically concretized in a particular performance, the processes of arithmetic are given a physical representation in a computing machine, the thought processes of the mind are given a physical embodiment in the workings of a brain. But, of course, the physical realizability or concretizability of such processes does not recategorize them as being physical processes in themselves.

Physical processes always possess some element of self-propulsion—if not active self-propagation then at least self-perpetuating inertia. To be sure, they are seldom (if ever) entirely autonomous and self-contained, impervious to all external influences and interferences. But they always do make some substantial self-engendered contribution to their own ongoing realization. Some element of reflexive self-orientation (self-realization, self-formation, self-perpetuation, and the like) is inherent in virtually every physical process, seeing that throughout nature everything tries to realize itself, to constitute itself as that which its inner impetus dictates its destiny to be. The basic drive or nisus the world's furnishings is not so much (as with Spinoza) one of self-preservation (*conatus se preservandi*) as one of self-realization, of bringing itself to its own fullest actualization (*conatus se realizandi*). Creative self-determination rules: Everywhere there are processes at work bringing heretofore nonexistent beings and modes of being to realization.

Processes effect changes. They make a difference in the world's scheme of things in actualizing a heretofore open, indeterminate future in ways that distinguish it for the determinate past. But processes also establish connections. The infant and the septuagenarian, the apple seed and the full-grown tree flowering in spring are connected, integrated, unified, and individuated into a single unit with its ongoing identity through the operation of a complex manifold of subordinate processes which together constitute the macroprocess that is the history of that person or tree. A process involves more than change as such. It is always a matter of *organized* variation—structured change is of the very nature of process. In particular, physical processes are interlinked with one another. They reach out in space and time to form a manifold of interconnectedness with smaller, subordinate processes always joining to form larger, superordinate ones. Natural processes thus organize one another into larger interconnected clusters—process organisms of sorts. Accordingly, process metaphysicians are given to conceptualizing nature in general—and physical nature in particular—in organic terms, owing to the tendency, at work everywhere in nature, for processes to cluster together in self-perpetuating systemic wholes. The world's processes are thus interconnected. They are stitches in the vast tapestry of a coherent system. Microprocesses combine in an all-inclusive fusion. And they replicate ongoingly across the cosmic landscape in an evolutionary connectedness. In process cosmology, all carbon atoms learn to behave like carbon atoms in somewhat the same way that in biology all camels learn to behave like camels: In each case it is a matter of breeding true to type.[1]

2. PROCESS AND EXISTENCE

The process approach provides a natural means for explaining the existence of the world's furnishings and affords an efficient instrumentability for the scientific understanding of the real. Consider the following discussion by C. G. Hempel:

> Why is there anything at all, rather than nothing? . . . But what kind of an answer could be appropriate? What seems to be wanted is an explanatory account which does not assume the existence of something or other. But such an account, I would submit, is a logical impossibility. For generally, the question "Why is it the case that *A*? is answered by "Because *B* is the case." . . . [*A*]*n answer to our riddle which made no assumptions about the existence of anything cannot possibly provide adequate*

grounds. . . . The riddle has been constructed in a manner that makes an answer logically impossible.[2]

This plausible-seeming line of argumentation has a severe shortcoming, for process ontology opens up a new approach to scientific explanation. It is important to distinguish appropriately between the *existence of things* and the *obtaining of facts*[3]—and supplementarily also between specifically substantival facts regarding existing things and nonsubstantival facts regarding *states of affairs* that are not dependent on the operation of preexisting things. We are here confronted with a principle of hypostatization predicated on the idea that on grounds of logical principle *the reason for anything must ultimately always inhere in the operations of things.*

The stance that is implicit in Hempel's argument is prominently explicit in much of the Western philosophical tradition. David Hume, for example, emphatically insisted that there is no feasible way in which an existential conclusion can be obtained from nonexistential premises.[4] The principle was also supported by philosophers of a very different ilk on the other side of the Channel, including Leibniz himself, who writes with characteristic explicitness that "the sufficient reason [of contingent existence] . . . must be outside this series of contingent things, and *must reside in a substance which is the cause of this series.*"[5] Such a view amounts to a thesis of genetic homogeneity that says (on analogy with the old but now surely untenable idea that "life must come from life") that "things must come from things" or "stuff must come from stuff" or "substance must come from substance."

At this point we have a prejudice as deeply rooted as any in Western philosophy—the idea that things can originate only from things, that nothing can come from nothing (*ex nihilo nihil fit*) in the sense that no *thing* can emerge from a thing-devoid condition.[6] Now, this somewhat ambiguous principle is quite unproblematic when construed to say that if the existence of something real has a correct explanation at all, then this explanation must pivot on something that is really and truly so. For, clearly, we cannot explain one *fact* without involving further *facts* to do the explaining. However, the principle becomes highly problematic when construed in the manner of the precept that "*things* must come from *things*," that *substances* must inevitably be invoked to explain the existence of *substances*. For we now become committed to the thesis that everything in nature has an efficient cause in some other natural thing that is its causal source, its reason for being.

That substance-requiring principle is thus eminently dubious. For, despite its surface appeal, the plausible-sounding idea that only substantial causes can have substantial effects has major problems. It presupposes that there must be a type homogeneity between cause and effect along the lines of the ancient Greek principle that "like must come from like." This highly problematic idea of genetic homogeneity has taken hard knocks in the course of modern science, which teaches that matter can come from energy, and living organisms from complexes of inorganic molecules. If such a principle fails as regards matter and life, need it hold for substance as such? The claim that it does so would need a very cogent defense. None has been forthcoming to date.

Is it indeed true that only things can engender things? Why must a ground of change always inhere in a thing rather than in a nonsubstantival "condition of things-in-general"? Must substance inevitably arise from substance—rather than, say, from a law or principle or "mere abstraction"of some sort?[7] Even to assert such a requirement is in effect to challenge its credentials. Why must the explanation of facts rest in the operation of *things*? To be sure, fact explanations must have inputs (*all* explanations must). Facts must root in facts. But why in thing-existential ones? A highly problematic bit of metaphysics is involved here. Dogmas about explanatory homogeneity aside, there is no discernible reason why an existential fact cannot be grounded in nonexistential ones and the existence of substantial things be explained on the basis of some nonsubstantival circumstance or principle. Once we give up the principle of genetic homogeneity and abandon the idea that existing things must originate in existing things, the whole enterprise of explanation assumes a different mien. Explanation can now proceed—in theory, at least—in terms of processes rooted in the operation of fields or forces that pervade nature at large and in their turn engender the particularized powers and potentialities of identifiable things.[8]

Modern physics is in many ways deeply congenial to a process approach. In particular, quantum theory has it that at the level of the very small there are no ongoing "material" *things* (substances, objects) at all in nature, no particulars with a continuing descriptive identity of their own; there are only patterns of process that exhibit stabilities. (The orbit-jump of an "electron" is not the mysterious transit of a well-defined physical *object* at all.) Only those stability-waves of continuous process provide for any sort of continuity of existence; the development of stable "things" begins at the sub-submicroscopic level with a buzzing proliferation of "events" that have little if any fixed nature in themselves but only exist in reciprocal interaction with each other. Such "objects" have no stable characteristics in and of themselves but only come to exhibit spatiotemporally stable aspects at the level of statistical aggregates. A process approach thus simplifies greatly the problem of securing a coherent view of nature.

In this regard, however, Whitehead's approach in process philosophy was somewhat flawed. For Whitehead insisted upon irreducibly atomic units of process—"actual occasions"—themselves altogether indecomposible and serving as basic units or building blocks out of which all larger processes are then constituted. This process atomism is certainly a theoretical possibility. But it is also a dubious proposition—and one that is rather at odds with the spirit of process philosophy. Why, after all, should process be seen as in discretized units? Whitehead's theory of processes as rooted in the aggregation of atomistic "actual occasions" is an unhappy concession to a thoroughly process-estranged point of view. Why should the succession of subordinate processes inevitably have to come to an end? It is far more appropriate to contemplate a Chinese box–like succession of larger processes enhancing over small ones: the poet's situation of larger fleas having ever smaller ones to bite 'em—ad infinitum. After all, if nature is indeed processual, then why should not its composition be processual "all the way through"? Why should there be ultimate particles of process that are nowise resolvable into more basic constituents? From the process point of view, it is surely only natural to see nature as a manifold of concatenated processes that admit—in principle—of decomposition into ever-smaller processual units; a pervasively structured manifold of micro- and macroprocess whose intricacy is unlimited and does not come to an end is a rock bottom of some sort that is itself exempt from the process of decomposition that we find at work everywhere else.

In this regard as in others, Teilhard de Chardin was a typical process philosopher. For him, "the universe is no longer a State but a Process."[9] As Teilhard saw it, nature everywhere strives to produce something new in this world's scheme of things. Nature is not something fixed and given; it is "a world that is ever *being born* instead of a world that is"[10]—change, development, and evolutionary emergence are the world's only pervasive and enduring features. We live in a world centering on a specious present that is ever in transit from a realized past to an open future: "Every particle of reality, instead of constituting a self-contained point in itself, extends from the previous fragment to the next along an inevitable thread running back to infinity."[11] And not only do natural processes produce "things," it is their no less crucial contribution to bring into being new types (species) and new patterns of order (laws). The evolutionary origination of new kinds is operative not in the biological realm above but throughout nature—at every level of detail and size (micro and macro alike).

Process metaphysics accordingly stresses the developmental aspect of the real in ways which natural science enables us to grasp more concretely. On its approach, primacy belongs to active (productive) nature (*natura naturans*) at the creative frontier of the innovative present over against the finished realm of accomplished fact (*natura naturata*). The temporal aspect of an ever-new present that gives embodiment to a novelty-enhancing manifold of possibility and potential through concretization into a body of realized actuality lies at the forefront of process philosophy's conception of the natural world. It is a position that insists on seeing nature as a manifold of processes—and a mixed manifold at that—one that includes sectors both of rigid causal determinism and open unforeseeability, since only a world that embodies chance and free choice can provide that "universe with elbow room" which William James envisioned as the indispensable setting of a satisfying human existence.

3. PROCESS AND THE LAWS OF NATURE

The salient idea of process philosophy is that the world consists of—and must, in consequence, be understood in terms of—changes rather than fixed stabilities. But from the time of Pythagoras, various philosophers have taught that while the world's *phenomena* may be ever-changing, the *laws* that govern the comportment of these changes are stable and fixed once and for all. Following the lead of C. S. Peirce, process metaphysics firmly rejects this contention. As it sees the matter, process invades the world's law-structure as well; the laws of nature, too, are merely transitory stabilities that emerge at one phase of cosmic history only to lapse from creation and give way to variant modes of operation in the fullness of time. And so, not only do the world's phenomena change but so do the natural laws that govern their modus operandi. On this perspective, the world's only pervasive permanence is change itself. Even the so-called laws of nature are themselves little more than islands of relative stability in a sea of process.

Such a processual view of natural law has important advantages. For a substance ontology is committed to seeing the physical world (nature) as a collection of substantial things or objects. And on this basis, it immediately faces the additional and vexing problem of accounting for the laws that coordinate the behavior of its things. (How do all the hydrogen atoms there are scattered through the vastness of space learn how to behave like hydrogen atoms?) As substance philosophy has it, substances emerge under the aegis of laws (and thus have a natural explanation), but the laws are ever-fixed and "given" in ways that exclude any genetic account and allow only the stonewalling explanation: "That's just the way it is." No natural explanation of physical lawfulness is available

on such an approach; its only—and by tradition familiar—
resort is to some extra- or supranatural agency to impose lawfulness on the substances that are supposed to constitute
nature.

But by seeing the world as a matrix of process (and
indeed often self-implicating process) we secure straightaway
a coherent conceptualization of nature in a way that removes
such difficulties. For the idea of lawful order, of programmed
development, is inherent in the very concept of a process.
Moreover, processes concatenate and propagate—the diffusion of processes is itself a process. The ontology of lawfulness
is thus provided for. And a basis is laid for its epistemology as
well. For it is only natural and to be expected that intelligent
creatures should be in a position to *understand* the world's
processes in some measure, seeing that they themselves are a
nature-internal party to them, in that they participate in the
operations of nature by virtue of being component elements
thereof.

The fact is that neither the logic of object and predicate
nor even the grammar of subject and verb prevail in the language of nature. Rather, it is the mathematical language of
differential equations that best represents its language of
process. In this regard as in so many others, Leibniz had
insight far beyond his time. Important though verbalized language may be (and he stressed that it is *very* important), it is
nevertheless the mathematical language of process—of transformation functions and differential equations—that is essential for representing the world's physical realities. This is a fact
of which process philosophers have not made as much as
they ought, although it is something of which Whitehead,
himself a first-rate mathematician, was keenly aware.

C. S. Peirce thought of laws of nature as settled but
acquired habits—stable modes of operation that the universe
has acquired over time and, once developed, retained for good.
But given the prominence of chance and chaos in contemporary science, it might be more plausible to see the laws of
nature as themselves constituting pervasive processes, consisting in transitory (and thus mortal) regularity patterns that
hold for large sections of space-time and then give way, be it

cataclysmically or gradually, to different process patterns. On such a view, the machinery of process provides a vehicle for the engendering of order in place of potential chaos.

But how can order manage to preempt disorder? In theory, there are three principal ways:

- by *imposition* through some sort of causative agency acting ab extra
- by some sort of external *persuasion* (à la Plato's *Timaeus*)
- by some sort of *internal development,* some intrinsically generated mode of evolution-analogous emergence.

Process metaphysics rejects the first two (externally initiated) alternatives. The economies of immanentism lead it to abandon such extraneous factors and forces. For one thing, recourse to a process of internal development is itself a natural and self-potentiating resource of process philosophizing. Moreover, in the setting of a natural philosophy, supranaturalism must always bear a negative aspect. Accordingly, process metaphysics looks to a world-internal—and, indeed, a process-internal—origination of order. After all, order as such has an inherent tendency to self-perpetuation and self-propagation. Once order comes into being (in however unforeseeable and fortuitous a way) it tends to be self-potentiating, given the self-propulsive nature of most forms of natural process.[12]

To be sure, the forces of destabilization are at work, too. Indeterminism, unpredictability, and the emergence of novelty are all crucial to the process metaphysicians' view of things. But what they envision as central is not so much the organization of new things or types of things, but the ongoing emergence of new modes of comportment—new types of process.

Process metaphysics accordingly inclines to the view that cosmic evolution itself exhibits the emergence of more and more complex and elaborate forms of order: in the sequential development of materials for an ongoing series of sciences: plasma physics, particle physics, chemistry, biology, sociology, and so on. Cosmic development is the unfolding of ever more complex concatenations of process. And the crux of a process philosophy of nature is the conception that physical reality is itself one vast, all-encompassing megaprocess consisting of a virtually endless concentration of subordinate subprocesses—a Chinese nesting of box within box, as it were.

Beginning with Leibniz, processists reject a departmentalized world that has separate compartments for physical, biological, and psychological sectors of nature. They regard all existence as prismatically many-sided. For them, in general, reality at every level—from subatomic to cosmic—exhibits processes of all natural orders, however much more prominent some may be than others. Even atoms have their "mental" (information-processing) aspect, and even the cosmos as a whole has its "organic" aspect as a self-engendering and self-sustaining system. Process thinkers incline to blend and blur such categorical difference by regarding them as differences in degree rather than in kind. They tend to the view that the different categories of natural understanding "mix it up" throughout all sectors of nature.

4. SPACE–TIME

Process metaphysicians regard the natural world as one vast interconnected manifold of process. But once a process commences, it has a formative impact both in its own future development and on the development of other processes. To be sure, a process can generally be aborted by "external" events (e.g., a germinating plant being eaten by a passing deer). But if all goes well—as it normally or frequently does—the process takes its course in line with its own internal impetus. In this sense, a process-laden world provides wide scope for formative self-determination. The world's processes exhibit a substantial degree of spontaneity of self-potentiation, generally exhibiting a capacity to develop their own structure on a produce-as-you-go basis. Processes throughout nature intertwine and interrelate; they run up against one another in one vast but cohesive manifold of occurrence. And the spatiotemporality of nature is nothing but a characteristic feature of this manifold—it forms the context of processes in the presence of one another. It is part and parcel of the processually structured make-up of that all-inclusive megaprocess represented by the origination, development, and (putative) decay of the entire universe.

Process philosophy sees every natural process as having an inherently spatiotemporal connection, and has it that the ramifications of space and time encompass all of nature. But there are two ways of conceiving of space-time: (1) as a container within (or a stage upon) which natural processes transpire, or (2) as itself an actual complex or state of process, a process-manifold of sorts that is itself constituted by the interlocking structure of individual process. The first perspective sees space-time as independent of the processes that happen with it, the second as itself an aspect of natural process, as a resultant part of the natural interrelatedness of such processes. And process philosophy adopts the second view. Its exponents abandon the Newtonian hypostatization of space and time, seen as fixed stable containers for nature's things— a view that goes back to the Atomists of Greek antiquity and plays into the hands of substance philosophy. Instead, they adopt, with Whitehead, Leibniz's relativistic conception of space-time as a manifold defined by the structure of natural process itself (coordinate with the diffusion of electromagnetic signal-processes in nature). Such an approach is tailor made for the process point of view. And process metaphysics accordingly sees space-time not as a matrix of order imposed on natural process from without by the structure of a process-independent stage on which natural processes must play themselves out. Space-time is itself part of the overall law structure that nature's processes internalize. Time is typified by the outward flow of a wave pattern, and space by the stability of a configuration of standing waves. Space and time are, in the final analysis, no more—but also no less—than inherent aspects of the characteristic interrelationship of physical processes.

For processists, then, space-time itself is simply a structural facet or feature of the modus operandi of cosmic processes. Nature's processes are interrelated and interlinked by patterns of causal connection, and space-time in itself is a manifold of such patterns—a feature of the exclusions and interference of such processes. (One cannot put two different things into the same place, nor can one thing exhibit different features at one and the same time. Such exclusions and improbabilities serve to give definition to space-time.) Space and time are accordingly not static containers that set the stage for nature's processes, but are themselves process-constituted as aspects or features of the structural role of nature's processes. Their ultimate metaphysical status is not process-independent but rather process-constituted, their structure being determined through processes of interrelation that manifest their inherently processual basis.

This perspective puts process philosophers in opposition to the time concept of classical, Newtonian physics. Thus, James and Bergson insist that the linear time of Newton's physics is not part of nature but an abstraction; all real time exhibits breadth and duration; it comes in intervals. Process philosophers incline to extend this view from biological and psychological ("lived, experienced") time to the time of physics as well. They insist that any process takes its time (however short); there are no punctiform, instantaneous processes. Regarding this as the salient lesson of Zeno's paradoxes, process philosophers count it as a central feature of their own position.

Accordingly, process metaphysics insists on the present status of temporality as manifesting the dynamism of an ever-innovative present. George Herbert Mead typified the processists' special stress upon the role of the present as representing the emergent frontier of existence in the world's process of development. "Reality," he emphasized, "exists in a present."[13] Each present is a locus of emergence that yields novelty in its actual being. Citing as an example the flash of a meteor as it burns up upon entering the earth's atmosphere Mead said, "That which marks a present is its becoming and its disappearing."[14] He saw the structure of time as based on the modus operandi of an ever-transitory present. The past is in large measure a reconstruction from the present; the future an anticipation of the present. Mead specifically rejected Bergson's view that the present somehow accumulates all the past: "The present," he said, "does not carry any such burden with it."[15] Instead of total accumulation, the past merely serves as a generative condition of the present. "The actual passage of reality is in the passage of one present into another, where alone is reality, and a present which has merged in another is not a past. Its reality is always that of a present."[16] In the natural philosophy of process, the idea of time stands correlative with a transient present of ever-changing creativity. Time is so central and important in process philosophy because temporality is the definitive characterizing feature of the processual nature of the real. To be real is to occupy a place in the order of time.

Is the origin and nature of our processual world itself explicable? Processists part ways here. Some invoke the will of God (Leibniz). Others see things happening by an inner impetus of not so much *logical* as *ontological* necessity (Hegel). Yet others acknowledge the operation of brute chance (Laplace). And some allow matters to rest in the lap of mystery, agreeing with John Dewey: "We can account for a change by relating it to other changes, but existences we have to accept for just what they are. . . . The mystery is that the world is as it is."[17] But sophisticated processists join forces with C. S. Peirce here. Given that human intelligence is a resource developed over time by creatures that are themselves an evolved part of nature, our capacity to understand the world should not be seen as all that surprising.[18] Here as elsewhere, process philosophy can and does make the most of a recourse to the evolutionary process.

5. The Quantum Aspect

As Whitehead's own reaction shows,[19] the rise of quantum theory put money in the process philosopher's bank account. The classical conception of an atom was predicated on the principle that "by definition, atoms cannot be cut up or broken into smaller parts," so that "atom-splitting" was, from the traditional point of view, simply a contradiction in terms. Here the demise of classical atomism brought on by the dematerialization of physical matter in the wake of quantum theory did much to bring aid and comfort to a process-oriented metaphysics. For matter in the small, as quantum physics conceives it, is not a Rutherfordian planetary system of particle-like objects but a collection of fluctuating processes organized into stable structures (insofar as there is, indeed, stability at all) by statistical regularities—that is, by regularities of comportment at the level of aggregate phenomena.

The quantum view of reality has accordingly led to the unravelling of that classical atomism which has, from the start, been paradigmatic for substance metaphysics. For quantum theory taught that, at the microlevel, what was usually deemed a physical *thing*, a stably perduring object, is itself no more than a statistical pattern—a stability wave in a surging sea of process. Those so-called enduring things come about through the emergence of stabilities in statistical fluctuations.

Twentieth-century physics has thus turned the tables on classical atomism. Instead of very small things (atoms) combining to produce standard processes (windstorms and such), modern physics envisions very small processes (quantum phenomena) combining in their modus operandi to produce standard things (ordinary macro-objects).

The quantum view of the world is inherently probabilistic—indeed, it has trouble coming to terms with concrete definiteness (with the "collapse of the wave packet" problem). And this, too, is congenial to processists, seeing that process philosophy rejects a pervasive determinism of law-compulsion. Processists see the laws of nature as imposed from below rather than above—as servants rather than masters of the world's existents. Process metaphysics envisions a limit to determinism that makes room for creative spontaneity and novelty in the world (be it by way of random mutations with naturalistic processists or purposeful innovation with those who incline to a theologically teleological position).

Moreover, process philosophers have reason to favor quantum physics over relativistic physics. For relativity sees space-time as a block that encompasses all real events concurrently, leaving the time differentiation of earlier/later to be supplied from the subjective resources of observers relative to their own mode of emplacement within the grand scheme of things. Special relativity with its preoccupation with time-invariant relationships in effect suppresses time as a factor in physical reality and relegates it to the penumbral status of a subjective phenomenon. This serves to explain why Whitehead sought to provide a new theoretical basis to relativity theory and reconstrue space-time, as well as the conception of other physical objects, as being constructions made from "fragmentary individual experiences."[20] Processes are not the machinations of stable things; things are the stability patterns of variable processes. All such perspectives of modern physics at the level of fundamentals dovetail smoothly into the process approach.

6. Process Philosophy and Evolutionary Optimism

Evolution is thus an emblematic and paradigmatic process for process philosophy. For not only is evolution a process that makes philosophers and philosophy possible, but it provides a clear model for how processual novelty and innovation comes into operation in nature's self-engendering and self-perpetuating scheme of things. Evolution, be it of organism or of mind, of subatomic matter or of the cosmos as a whole, reflects the pervasive role of process which philosophers of this school see as central both to the nature of our world and to the terms in which it must be understood. Change pervades nature. Process at once destabilizes the world and is the cutting edge of advance to novelty. And evolution of every level—physical, biological, and cosmic—carries the burden of the work here. But does it work blindly?

On the issue of purposiveness in nature, process philosophers divide into two principal camps. On the one side is the naturalistic (and generally secularist) wing that sees nature's processuality as a matter of an inner push or nisus to something new and different. On the other side is the teleological (and often theological) wing that sees nature's processuality as a matter of teleological directness toward a positive destination. Both agree in according a central role to novelty and innovation in nature. But the one (naturalistic) wing sees this in terms of chance-driven randomness that leads away from the settled formulations of an established past, while the other (teleological) sees this in terms of a goal-directed purposiveness preestablished by some value-geared directive force.[21]

Process philosophy correspondingly has a complex, two-sided relationship with the theory of evolution. For secular, atheological processists, evolution typifies the creative workings of a self-sustaining nature that dispenses with the services of God. For theological processists like Teilhard de Chardin, evolution exhibits God's handwriting in the book of nature.[22] But processists of all descriptions see evolution not only as a crucial instrument for understanding the role of intelligence in the world's scheme of things but also as a key aspect of the world's natural development. And, more generally, the evolutionary process has provided process philosophy with one of its main models for how large-scale collective processes (on the order of organic development at large) can inhere in and result from the operation of numerous small-scale individual processes (on the order of individual lives), thus accounting for innovation and creativity also on a macrolevel scale.

But there is one further complexity here. Where human intelligence is concerned, biological evolution is undoubtedly Darwinian, with teleologically blind natural selection operating with respect to teleologically blind random mutations. Cultural evolution, on the other hand, is generally Teilhardian, governed by a rationally guided selection among purposefully devised mutational variations.[23] Taken in all, cognitive evolution involves both components, superimposing rational selection on biological selection. Our cognitive capacities and faculties are part of the natural endowment we owe to biological evolution. But our cognitive methods, procedures, standards, and techniques are socioculturally developed resources that evolve through *rational* selection in the process of cultural transmission through successive generations. Our cognitive hardware (mechanisms and capacities) develops through Darwinian natural selection, but our cognitive software (the methods and procedures by which we transact our cognitive business) develops in a Teilhardian process of rational selection that involves purposeful intelligence-guided variation and selection. Biology produces the instrument, so to speak, and culture writes the music—where obviously the former powerfully constrains the latter. (You cannot play the drums on a piano.)

The ancient Greeks grappled with the question; Is anything changeless, eternal, and exempt from the seemingly all-destructive ravages of time? Rejecting the idea of eternal material atoms, Plato opted for eternal changeless universals ("form," "ideas") and the Stoics for eternal, changeless laws. But the world-picture of modern science has seemingly blocked these solutions. For, as it sees the matter, species (natural kinds) are also children of time, not changelessly present but ever-changingly emergent under the aegis of evolutionary principles. The course of cosmic evolution brings nature's laws also within the orbit of process, endowing these laws with a developmental dimension (where, after all, was genetics in the microsecond after the Big Bang?). For process philosophy, nothing is eternal and secure from the changes wrought by time and its iron law that everything that comes into being must perish, so that mortality is omnipresent and death's cold hand is upon all of nature—laws as well as things.

However, process philosophy does not see this gloomy truth as the end of the story. For this doctrine has always looked to evolutionary theory to pull the plum of collective progress from the pie of distributive mortality. In the small— item by item—nature's processes are self-cancelling: What arises in the course of time perishes in the course of time. But nevertheless the overall course of processual change tends to the development of an ever richer, more complex and sophisticated condition of things on the world's ample stage. For there are processes and processes: processes of growth and decay, of expanding and contracting, of living and dying. Recognizing that this is so, process philosophy has always accentuated the positive and worn a decidedly optimistic mien. For it regards nature's microprocesses as components of an overall macroprocess whose course is upward rather than downward, so to speak. Hitching its wagon to the star of a creative evolutionism, process philosophy sees nature as encompassing creative innovation, productive dynamism, and an emergent development of richer, more complex and sophisticated forms of natural existence.

To be sure, there are, in theory, both productive and destructive processes, degeneration and decay being no less prominent in nature than growth and development. Historically, however, most process philosophers have taken a positive view and have envisioned a close relationship between *process* and *progress*. For them, this relationship is indicated by the macroprocess we characterize as evolution. At every level of world history—the cosmic, the biological, the social, the intellectual—process philosophers have envisioned a developmental dynamic in which later is *better*, somehow superior in being more differentiated and sophisticated. Under the influence of Darwinian evolutionism, most process philosophers have envisioned a course of temporal development within which value is somehow survival-facilitative so that the arrangements which do succeed in establishing and perpetuating themselves will, as a general tendency, manage to have done so because they represent actual improvements in one way or another. (A decidedly optimistic tenor has prevailed throughout process philosophy.[24])

After all, differentiation is sophistication; detail is enrichment. Someone who merely sees a bird does not see as much as the person who sees a finch, and that person in turn does not see as much as the person who sees a Darwin finch. The realization and enhancement of detail bestows not just complexification as such but also sophistication. As process philosophy sees it, the world's processuality involves not only change but improvement—the evolutionary realization—at large and on the whole, of what is not only different but also in some way better. Accordingly, novelty and fruitfulness compensate for transiency and mortality in process philosophy's scheme of things.

Process philosophy centers around the idea of a natural processual dialectic that brings innovation and novelty into being at all points on the compass. But its capacity to depict this course of development as not just a matter of change but one of *superiority* in matters of complexity and sophistication is entirely dependent upon the use that processists make of the explanatory resources of evolutionary theory.[25]

7. VALIDATION

How is reliance on the process approach in the philosophy of nature to be validated? What is it that speaks for taking this particular line? The answer lies in a complex negotiation of process thought with natural science. Not that process metaphysics is a part or consequence of natural science as such—metaphysics is always a supplementation to rather than an extraction from natural science. Instead, what is at issue is a matter of interpretation and harmonization, of assessing which of the metaphysical alternatives accords most smoothly and naturally and efficiently with the world-picture that natural science puts at our disposal.[26] And as one reviews the principal building blocks of a process philosophy of nature—pervasive processuality, causal interrelationship and lawful development, processual structure and organization, spatiotemporal structurization, self-development though "organic" organization, innovation by evolutionary emergence, and the rest—it is vividly brought to view that the characteristic perspectives of a process philosophy of nature all cohere and harmonize with the understanding of physical processes that contemporary science delivers into our hands.

To be sure, at the level of generality of a rather elevated abstraction, a process philosophy of nature and a traditional substance philosophy of nature along the lines of a classical atomism exhibit some similarities—for example, both see the world as a manifold of identifiable things that are identifiable particulars located in space-time and interacting under the aegis of causal laws. But the crucial fact is that each and every one of the conceptions involved here is interpreted differently in the two camps. With respect to "manifold of things," "identifiable particulars," "space-time location," and "causal interaction" are provided with a totally different interpretation. And for process philosophy, the crucial consideration is that its own interpretations are throughout better attuned to the spirit and letter of contemporary natural science than those of its substantialist rival. Indeed, process philosophy sees this factor as so pivotal an asset as to stake upon it the main burden of its claims to acceptability.[27]

6

Process and Persons

SYNOPSIS

(1) Because of its resistance to accommodation in a substance ontology, the self or ego has been a stumbling block for Western philosophy. The process approach offers a far more promising prospect here. (2) Process philosophy is not committed to denying materialism. Even if mental processes are causally rooted in physical ones (a view subject to the Scots verdict of not proven), the fact remains that these two are fundamentally different in their experiential nature and hermaneutic character. (3) Individual human life is a process geared to the "life cycle" of homo sapiens. Our lives are lived on borrowed time and like all processes have a beginning and an end. (4) And human history at large is also a matter of process. (5) But while in a world of process all things—short of the entire whole itself—are transitory, human arrangements included, this fact does not destroy their value.

1. Difficulties of the Self and the Process Approach to Persons

The utility of the process approach in philosophical psychology also deserves recognition. The self, or ego, has always been a stumbling block for Western philosophy because personhood resists accommodation within its favored framework of substance ontology. It is somewhere between difficult and infeasible to come to satisfying terms with the idea that "the self" is a *thing* (substance), and that whatever takes place in "my mind" and "my thoughts" is a matter of the activity of a substantial item of a certain sort (be it a physical brain or a somehow substantial mind).

If one is committed to conceiving of a *person* within the framework of a classical substance metaphysic, then one is going to be impelled inexorably toward the materialist view that the definitive facet of a person is his body and its doings. For of everything that appertains to us, it is clearly one's *body* that is most readily assimilated to the substance paradigm. It is instinctive to recall David Hume's ventures into self-apprehension in this context:

> From what (experiential) impression could this idea [of *self*] be derived? This question is impossible to answer without a manifest contradiction and absurdity; and yet it is a question which must necessarily be answered, if we would have the idea of self pass for clear and intelligible. . . . For my part, when I enter most intimately into what I call *myself*, I always stumble on some particular perception or other, of heat or cold, light or shade, love or hatred, pain or pleasure. I never can catch *myself* at any time without a perception, and never can observe anything but the perception.[1]

Here Hume is perfectly right. Any such quest for *observational* confrontation with a personal core substance, a self or ego that constitutes the particular person that one is, is destined to end in failure. The only "things" about ourselves we can get hold of *observationally* is the body and its activities and sensations.

Yet it feels inappropriate and uncomfortable to conceptualize people (persons) as things (substances)—oneself above all—because we instinctively resist flat-out identification of our personality-endowed selves with our material bodies. Aristotle already bears witness to this difficulty of accommodating the self or soul into a substance metaphysics. It is, he tells us, the "substantial form," the entelechy of the body. However, this particular accommodation strategy led Aristotle into difficulties, because the self or soul is so profoundly unlike the other sorts of *entelechy* examples he was able to provide. And moreover, the only way he could put the idea to work was with reference to the soul's processual functions.

The substance approach is inherently uncongenial to personhood. People instinctively dislike being described in thing-classificatory terms. As J. P. Sartre remarked, a wrong-doer may be prepared to say, "I did this or that act," but will resist saying, "I am a thief," "I am a murderer."[2] Such attributions indicate a fixity of constitution that we naturally deem repugnant in relation to ourselves. People generally incline to see themselves and their doings in processual terms as agents—as productive sources of teleological, agency-purposive activities geared to the satisfaction of needs and wants as they appear in the circumstances of the moment. In application to ourselves, at any rate, a static thing-oriented perspective is naturally distasteful to us, seeing that its stolid substantiality makes for a fixity that simply does not square with the character of our experience.

From the angle of a process metaphysics, however, the situation has a very different look. For while we may have difficulties in apprehending experientially what we *are*, we clearly have no comparable difficulty in experiencing what we *do*. By virtue of our capacity for conscious awareness, our bodily and mental activities lie open to experiential apprehension. Our doings and undergoings (either individually or grouped into talents, skills, capabilities, traits, dispositions, habits, inclinations, and tendencies to action and inaction) are, after all, what characteristically constitutes us as individuals, and there is no problem with experiential access to these processes and patterns of process. What makes my experience mine is not some peculiar qualitative character that it exhibits but simply its forming part of the overall ongoing macroprocess that defines, constitutes, and characterizes my life in those of its dimensions that are, in principle, cognitively accessible to myself and to others.

And so, once we conceptualize the core "self" of a person as a unified manifold of actual and potential process—of action and capacities, tendencies, and dispositions to action (both physical and psychical)—then we obtain a concept of personhood that renders the self or ego experientially accessible, seeing that experiencing itself simply *consists* of such processes. As process philosophy sees it, the unity of a person resides neither in the physical body as such nor in the psychic unity of custom and memory but in a synoptic unity of process. On a process-oriented approach, the self or ego—the particular individual that one is—is simply a megaprocess, a structured system of processes, a cohesive and (relatively) stable center of activity agency.[3] For processists, our sense of self is the glimmering insight of part into the whole to which it sees itself as belonging. The unity of person is a unity of experience—the coalescence of all of one's diverse microexperience as part of one unified macroprocess. (It is the same sort of unity of process that links each minute's level into a single overall journey.) The crux of this approach is the shift in orientation from substance to process—from a substantive unity of hardware, of physical machinery, to a processual unity of software, of programming or mode of functioning. A body or a brain is, after all, something we *have*, while a life is something we *live* and a personality is something we *exhibit*. Here process comes to the fore.

People are constituted as the individuals they are through their doings, their history: one is the individual that one is by nature of the macroprocess that integrates the microprocesses constituting one's life and career. The unity of process is a narrative unity that deals not in fixed things but rather in materials that—like the artifacts in a collection of memorabilia or in a museum—cry out to be "brought to life" by accounts that portray a coherent story. In the subjective experience of individuals the clearly processual character of William James's "stream of consciousness" is a phenomenologically notable feature of everyday experience. As Dewey insisted, people are best understood in temporal and processual terms:

> Take the individual Abraham Lincoln at one year, at five years, at ten years, at thirty years of age, and imagine everything later wiped out, no matter how minutely his life is recorded up to the date set. It is plain beyond the need of words that we then have not his biography but only a fragment of it, while the significance of that fragment is undisclosed. For he did not just exist in a time

which externally surrounded him, but time was the heart of his existence. Temporal seriality is the very essence, then, of the human individual. It is impossible for a biographer in writing, say the story of the first thirty years of the life of Lincoln, not to bear in mind his later career. Lincoln as an individual *is* a history; any particular event cut off from that history ceases to be part of his life as an individual. As Lincoln is a particular development in time, so is every other human individual. Individuality is the uniqueness of the history, of the career, not something given once for all at the beginning which then proceeds to unroll as a ball of yarn may be unwound. Lincoln made history. But it is just as true that he made himself as an individual in the history he made.[4]

Such an approach wholly rejects the thing-ontologists' view of a person as an *entity* existing separately from its actions, activities, and experiences.

The salient advantage of such a processual view of the self as an internally complex process of "leading a life (of a certain sort)"—with its natural division into a varied manifold of constituent subprocesses—is that it does away with the need for a mysterious and experientially inaccessible unifying substantial *object* (on the lines of Kant's "transcendental ego") to constitute a self out of the variety of its experiences. The unity of self comes to be seen as a unity of process—of one large megaprocess that encompasses many smaller ones in its make-up. We arrive at a view of mind that dispenses with the Cartesian "ghost in the machine" and looks to the unity of mind as a unity of functioning—of operations rather than operators. People are defined as the individuals they are through their active careers.

And this processual approach carries over naturally from persons to their minds. "The mind" is now not construed as being a substance of some (rather peculiar) sort. Instead, it is seen as a processual unifier of the manifold of mental processes that constitute a particular mental life—a macroprocess that comprises and integrates a varied host of mental microprocesses. Process metaphysics accordingly sees the human mind also as a matrix of process—of all those mental activities of ours. Thinking and feeling in all their manifold dimensions is the mind's stock in trade. And a person's particular mind is constituted as such by its forming a complex within which all of those smaller-scale mental processes are embraced and integrated. These psychic processes need not always be conscious—our conscious thought-life is, after all, interrupted by periods of sleep and unconsciousness. But, as Leibniz already insisted, the ongoing self-identity of mind consists in a continuity of psychic process—even if it lies beneath the threshold of awareness.

At this stage, the perspective of process philosophy is drawn toward an existentialist turn. It displays an affinity to Sartre's idea that human life is a matter of self-definition—of using one's free will to endow one's life with purposes ("forming a project") and then living it out so as to thrust this mode of being into reality ("projecting it into being"). To be a human being is, on such a telling, a matter of process—of making (and thus becoming) oneself: "Man is exactly that which he makes of himself."[5] Existentialism, however, neglects the social dimension. For processists, this processual unity of the person has a distinctly social aspect. As it sees the matter, the self-definitional activity of persons proceeds in the context of interaction with one another. The processual dispositions that define a person as the individual he or she is preeminently include those dispositions that characterize the person as part of a social order of communicative interrelationships. As G. H. Mead stressed,[6] the community-sustaining role of communication among social beings such that it is effectively impossible to study them sensibly in isolation, abstracting from the interpersonal relations that shape virtually the whole spectrum of their activities.

Miguel de Unamuno says somewhere that Descartes got it backwards: that one is not a thinking being because one thinks but rather that one thinks because one is a thinking being—that instead of *Cogito, ergo sum res cogitans*, it should be *Sum res cogitans, ergo cogito*.[7] But this is not so. Descartes's reversal of Scholasticism's substance-first perspective is perfectly in order, based on the sound idea that activity comes first ("*Im Anfang war die Tat*")—that what we do defines what we are. The fundamentality of psychic process for the constitution of a self was put on the agenda of modern philosophy by Descartes, although, unfortunately, he took too substance-oriented a view of a person—as his use of *res* (thing) indicates.

Leibniz went even further in generalizing the view that agency defines the agent. Proceeding along Cartesian lines of thought, he saw the unity of the self as a unity of process, taking its individuality to consist in a unified characteristic mode of agency in perceiving the world. He too still coordinated substances and persons. However, Leibniz shrewdly reversed Descartes's perspective. Instead of seeing a person as a thing (substance), he proposed to conceive of substances on analogy with persons. Accordingly, the self was, for Leibniz, paradigmatic for substance in general. In effect, Leibniz's monadology took the Cartesian process approach to the personal self and *universalized* it to encompass substance in general. As Leibniz saw it, a substance, like a self, is not really a "thing" of some sort but a center of action. In this regard as in so many others, Leibniz had insight far beyond his time.

For process philosophy, then, the conscious and unconscious experience that constitutes human life not only is a form of process but is itself emblematic of process, affording a paradigmatic—and particularly vivid—illustration of what process is all about.[8] And this involvement with process projects us into an ever-unfolding future. Futurition is not only something we witness in nature (as when the throbbing locomotive pushes its way into its future even as it pushes its way along the track) but also something we witness in ourselves whenever we realize and recognize that with each deliberate action we engender some possibilities at the cost of eliminating others. Our constant confrontation with the unknown—with a future that is always, to some extent, uncertain and unpredictable—is a fundamental feature of *human experiential reality* even if reality as such (whatever that might be!) is a *totum simul*.

On this basis, the Humean complaint—"One experiences feeling this and doing that, but one never experiences *oneself*"—is much like the complaint of the person who says, "I see him picking up that brick and mixing that batch of mortar and troweling that brick into place, but I never see him building a wall." Even as "building the wall" just exactly is the complex process that is *composed* of those various activities, so—from the process point of view—one's self just is the complex process *composed* of those various physical and psychic experiences and actions in their systemic interconnection.

Whitehead's process atomism of ultimate microconstituents ("actual occasions") borrows trouble for him and creates avoidable difficulties for his metaphysics.[9] Process philosophy is better served by a theory of processual levels that treat processes as existing in an interpenetrating order of levels of scale (much as with waves in water). Personal identity, in particular, meets with grave problems when approached as a construction of discrete elements. But when seen as a superordinated process embracing various smaller-scale, subordinate processes, most of the problems vanish.

Then, too, the process approach has the advantage when it comes to dealing with nonnatural persons. A partnership, a corporation, a government do not easily lend themselves to a substantialist conceptualization within a substance-oriented approach. But from a processist approach they can be construed, quite naturally, as processual complexes whose operation, in their turn, have impact-consequences for the occurrence of other processes.

The process-based approach in philosophical psychology doubtless has difficulties of its own. But they pale in significance when compared to those of the traditional substantival approach.

2. MIND AND MATTER IN PROCESSUAL PERSPECTIVE

Whitehead inclined to regard all feeling as a nonrelational mode of awareness.[10] But the fact is that while some feelings are objectless (giddiness, nausea), others are propositionally oriented that-feelings (that something is out of place in the desk, that something unpleasant is about to happen). Such relationally cognitive feelings are psychic processes that relate subjective sentiment to a (putatively) objective state of the world in a way that introduces an at least purported objectivity upon the scene. And under the pressure of evolution these psychic processes are reality-coordinated, endowing even our emotional life with a cognitive element. Natural process as such provides the instrumentalities of thought/world coordination that render worries about "the mind–body problem" moot.

Charles Hartshorne has maintained that process philosophers must be idealists, seeing that "they find no reasonable explanation of 'matter' except as a form of the manifestation of 'mind.'"[11] But this is going a bit too far. Only if we do something very strange with the idea of "mind" will it be such that "matter is a manifestation *of* mind." But it is quite unproblematic to maintain that everything that is comprehended or explained or understood at all is indeed a manifestation to mind. Mind may or may not be *ontologically* essential to the existence of matter, but it is certainly essential to its identification, explanation, comprehension, and the like—all of which are mental processes. Clearly, our only cognitive access to matter is mind-mediated and thereby processual.

But are such mental processes not all reducible to physical ones—does not the domain of the mind reduce to that of the brain so that physical (physiological) processes emerge as all there is? Are there two sorts of processes at issue here (the physical and the mental) or, at bottom, only one? Large and frustratingly complex issues are at stake here. But, for present purposes, one relatively straightforward point stands out, namely, that the occurrence in mind-endowed beings of the interpreted environmental impacts that constitute our sensory experiences is simply one sort of natural process among others.

When we look at a printed letter —say this W—there are two different things at issue: the (physical) ink mark and the (interpreted) symbol that it engenders in a transaction with minds. There is just one *thing* at issue: the letter, that is, the ink mark operating as a symbol; but it functions in two contexts: the material and the mind-coordinated. Analogously, when we concern ourselves with the thought processes of a human individual, there are not two distinct objects, the brain and the mind; there is simply one item: the complex of processes constituting the brain that has both its physical (brain physiological) and its mental (meaning-geared) dimension. Mental and physical processes are not *reducible*, the one to the other; they are *coordinated* as different aspects of one unified whole. Process metaphysics takes the holistic route.

The brain and those of its cognitive operations that constitute the workings of what we designate as "mind" form an integral component of the diversified flow of natural processes—just another part of nature's processual machinations (although perhaps that "just" is not exactly just here, given the centrality of mind from our human point of view). And so the traditional epistemological problem of how thought can comprehend reality—of how minds can get an intellectual grasp on material nature—is resolved by seeing both mental and physical processes as part and parcel of nature's processual commerce. The Cartesian dualism of mind and matter is, on this perspective, profoundly mistaken in transmuting a distinction in processual modes (in modus operandi) into a substantive difference between two fundamentally different kinds of substance (the mental and the material). Mental and material operations can thus be seen as two modes of natural process at large, representing a difference in sort but not in kind.

Causal and conceptual priority reflect different and non-conflicting issues. Accordingly, even if one allows (as there is very good reason for doing) the idea that "mind and its works are the causal product of the operations of matter" *it does not follow* that "the mind and its works are *nothing but* matter and its operations." For—to reemphasize—causal production is one thing and conceptual understanding another. And from the conceptual (as distinguished from causal) point of view, mind is autonomous. Its operations may be *explained* causally but they can only be *understood* conceptually. From the point of view of hemeneutic explanation (intelligentibility), the operations of mind must be understood in their own experiential terms. (Electromagnetical vibrations are one thing, phenomenally experienced colors another.) When we are concerned with mental operations as such, it is the experienced products constituted in the course of mind/matter interaction, and not the causal mechanisms of their (presumptive) production, that are at issue.

It is thus important to keep in view the clear and far-reaching distinction between *conceptual* involvement or invocation on the one hand and *causal* involvement or invocation on the other. Raw materials (flour, sugar, etc.) are *causally* requisite for the cake: They must be at hand before the physical process of cake production can get under way. But there is nothing in the *concept* of a cake that says it must be made in this way: It is possible, at least in theory, that cake could be made of very different stuff. And thus these ingredients are not called for in the conceptual order: The concept of cake is not essentially flour-referring as that of a raisin is grape-referring (since raisins simply *are* dried grapes). A thing can be linked *causally* to virtually anything else (caterpillars and butterflies; cigarette smoking and cancer). To reemphasize: Causal explanation is one thing, meaning explanation another.

And so, even if mental operations were to turn out to be "merely" the causal product of physical ones—an issue that is clearly controversial—the fact remains that natural processes are fundamentally different in their experienced nature and hermeneutic character from the physical ones in which (as per present supposition) they have their causal origin. Even if brain processes have primacy over mental ones in the *causal* order, the situation is reversed in the *hermeneutical* order. For mental processes are pivotal here because not only do we understand them but we also experience them. However, this priority of mental over physical processes in the *epistemic/ hermeneutical* order does not prevent the prospect of there being a reverse priority in the *ontological* order, with the operations of mind causally rooted in those of matter. Even as persons are more than the machinations of bodies, so minds are more than the machinations of brains. Different conceptual categories are involved in the two spheres of discourse. It is the analytical issue of *what* we think of the world, not the explanatory issue of the causal goings-on that account for *how* we do so, that constitutes the focus of concern when mental processes are seen as fundamental.

3. HUMAN LIFE AS A PROCESS: THE GENERAL IDEA OF A LIFE CYCLE

A person is evidentiated as a mind-activated being in a dual manner. For oneself, this substantiation proceeds through reflexive self-consciousness and memory which integrate the subjective immediacy of experience, forming both a cognitive sector of information and an affective sector of integrated enjoyment, satisfaction, and suffering. For others, this evidential constituting proceeds through interactions that also have a cognitive sector and a sector of affective involvement (sympathy, empathy, etc.). The "self," the human person, is accordingly best seen not as a substance or being (a thing of some sort) but as an experience-integrating life process of the human mode, the concrete realization of a developmental sequence comprising childhood, youth, maturity, and, finally, old age. To be sure, this characteristic line of development may—as with any process—be cut short (by Aristotelian privation or by uncooperative chance). But if all goes well it unfolds in a programmed sequence coordinated through a developmental (processual) unity of successive occurrence. As processists see it, a person not only *has* a developmental career but is individuated by it as the particular individual that he or she is. (Leibniz saw this as a matter of a person's individuation via a "complete individual concept.")

When individuating persons in our encounters with other people, one of the most basic perspectives is to view an individual in terms of his or her career. Human existence in this mortal sphere always presents us with an ever-changing situation. And the "outlook" of each successive age category looks very different. Altered planning horizons come into play. Children "have their whole lives before them" and incline to think that they will go on forever. The young live in a thought-world of unimpeded possibilities—as exemplified in teenage "day dreaming." The middle-aged inhabit a world of action and activity (of "making their way in the world") and are attracted toward the *carpe diem* outlook characteristic of midlife crises. The elderly approach the end of the tether of their potential. For them, the exercise of control and the enjoyment of the fruits of power is—where available—a cardinal good. The very old tend to glance backward and direct their future-oriented arrangements toward the *après nous* of their posterity.

The temporal transit through life's journey is associated with constantly changing views of prospects and possibilities. We think of a lifetime not only as an extent of temporal duration but also as a succession of definite stages. We view life in terms not just of a life *span* but of a life *cycle*. From hoary antiquity onward, literary tradition sees this in terms of an analogy to the seasons of a year; analogizing childhood to spring, youth to summer, maturity to autumn, and old age to winter. The medievals, habituated more to the diurnal ritual of the ecclesiastical day than to the agrarian cycle of the year, preferred a different analogy: the morning of childhood and youth, the midday of maturity, the evening of old age, and the coming of the eternal night where no man can work. (This set a theme to which the book of hours gave endless variations.)

Age classification proceeds in terms of a series of developmental stages, demarcated by "phase-transitions" that represent "milestones" in human development: capacity for speech (around 1–2 years of age), capacity for reproduction, or *biological* adulthood (around 10–13), capacity for self-management or *social* adulthood (around 18–21), onset of marked physical decline (around 55). These successive "milestones" represent phase transitions that constitute boundary crossings between the major successive stages of life. They are "rites of passage," as it were, through which we move from one of life's phases to the next.

From the human point of view, then, few processes are more significant than that of personal maturation and aging that represents a life cycle. Nothing about ourselves, save our identity itself, is stable and fixed; from the instant of our coming into this world we are caught up in the life-cycle process. It is a salient fact of philosophical anthropology that the unity of a person is a unity of process and that, while a name or number may *individuate* us in the sense of distinguishing us from others, what actually identifies us or the individual we are is our *career*—the overall matrix of process in which we are caught up. And for better or worse, the inescapable fact is that our lives are lived on borrowed time and, like all processes, have a beginning and an end.

But does the processual view of persons not wreak havoc with issues of moral responsibility? If we do not have recourse to substantial persons with their presumed essential transtemporal identities but replace this by something as impermanent as transitory processes, then how can one reasonably hold the person of today responsible for yesterday's transgressions?

Complaints of this nature rest on a mistaken view of the matter. It is nowise necessary that processes as such have to be brief, fleeting, and ephemeral. Process comes in all shapes and sizes. There are the substantive processes that constitute the being of a particle whose half-life may be a matter of nanoseconds, and there are the aeon-long cosmic processes that constitute the being of stars and galaxies. And in between come those undersized processes that constitute the career of animals—rational and moral agents included. The processual, career-connected nature of a particular person's life does nothing to impede that integrity and perduring identity of individuality that is characteristic of particular individual agents. And so transtemporal identity of agency is quite sufficient to provide a basis for personal responsibility.

4. HISTORICAL PROCESS

Let us turn from individuals to collectivities. After all, human history also is a matter of process.

A particularly important sector of process thought is represented by those who hold to a generalized theory of the structure of history. For societies no less than for individuals, our expectations for the future are inevitably grounded in our views of the past, for past and future are to be seen as connected parts of one ongoing historic process. (And in any event we have no basis of information for judging the future apart from the past and present.)

As regards the inherent structural trends and tendencies of history, there have been six major views:

- *progressive:* Matters are moving to a new and totally different—and better—order of things. (Enlightenment thinkers, Kant, Hegel, Comte, Marx, Utopian speculation, G.B. Shaw, Edward Ballamy)
- *retrogressive:* Matters are moving back to an older and inferior order of things. (Max Nordau, *Fin de siècle* theorists)
- *declivitous:* Matters are in an ongoing process of decay. (Xenophanes and other ancient thinkers)
- *stabilitarian:* Fundamentally, things remain pretty much the same over the course of time. (Ancient and medieval thinkers who took human beings to have a fixed essence and saw the history of societies to be inherent in this; also Fontenelle, Schopenhauer)
- *cyclic:* There is ongoing change; it does not have a fixed direction but moves in a repetitive pattern of ebbs and flows. (Ibn Khaldun, Vico, Nietzsche, Spengler, Toynbee)
- *stochastic:* Random fluctuations without any particular designatable pattern, simply now this, now that. (Carlyle)

The first of these, the theory of progress, has been the most popular and influential over the years, and has been particularly prominent since the origin of modern science in the sixteenth century. But it was prevalent already in classical antiquity, going back at least to Lucretius[12] and finding its clearest and most forceful exponent in Seneca. (Not that it was invariably shared—even in antiquity. Marcus Aurelius, for example, envisioned a fundamentally stable condition of affairs in which nothing is ever new for a well-experienced forty-year-old.[13])

Interestingly, all but the last of the aforementioned macrotheories see at least the general pattern of things to come as discernible in advance. After all, if history has any sort of definite overall shape or structure, then ipso facto the future becomes predictable—at least in its broad outlines. Most theorists of history—and most political philosophers, from Vico to Marx and beyond—have accordingly envisioned at least the broad course of human history as subject to forecast. Only in the present century have theories of randomness and chaos gained a place of prominence on the agenda.

For present purposes, however, the crucial fact is that each one of these rival positions sees the unfolding of human history as a process that has a discernible structure of a definite sort. (Even chaos, after all, is a mode of order.) And theories of historical process have accordingly been one of the most lively and influential sectors of process thinking of recent times, extending the idea of processual development from biological Darwinism in the biological realm to a social Darwinism in the human sphere. Any realistic approach to human history calls for a processual perspective. Human societies are what they are though their histories—objectively constituted and subjectively perceived. And as long as history is history as we know it, the processual perspective is so natural as to be effectively indispensable in this domain.

5. TRANSIENCY AND VALUE

"Here today and gone tomorrow." It lies in the nature of things that human life and all that goes with it is transitory. Time has ever been seen as the great devourer. Shakespeare speaks of the "tooth of time,"[14] echoing the Greek lyric poet, Simonides of Keos (d. 468 B.C.), who already spoke of "sharp-toothed time" two millennia before. A metaphysics of process need not necessarily regard reality with unalloyed optimism and in an altogether rosy light. There is no need for it to deny that nature has its dark side and includes negativity as well as positivity, evil as well as good. For one thing, the all-destructive impetus of time—of temporality and transience—casts its cold shadow over the domain of process and thus reaches out to encompass persons and their works. After all, processes in general are by nature ephemeral: Whatever has a beginning also has an end. In the domain of process, nothing is permanent except that domain itself—the collective maxiprocess that embraces all the rest. And transiency eventually means loss, since the passing of anything that is positive can itself be seen to be a negativity.

It deserves stress, however, that process philosophy's emphasis on transiency, change, and novelty does not—need not—reduce our human concerns to insignificance. It is simply inappropriate of most, always and everywhere, that "it just won't matter a hundred years hence." For one must not confuse value with permanency, importance with endurance. Clearly, what matters for importance is the validation that something makes a difference for the good in the overall scheme of things—a difference which turns on the condition of things *at the time*, then and there, and not in permanency of influence on the course of time as a whole.

Platonists meet the problem by seeing truth and value as themselves timeless. The fact of its having been beautiful remains even after the beautiful thing is gone. Without necessarily denying this, process philosophers, however, take a quite different line. The mechanism through which process philosophy has traditionally reconciled the dialectal tension between transiency and value is provided by the pivotal idea of an *evolutionary* process. The founding fathers of modern process philosophy—Peirce, James, Bergson, Whitehead, and the rest—were all profoundly influenced by the rise of Darwinian evolution. Now evolutionary development in all its various dimensions—cosmic, organic, cognitive—is not just a matter of mere change but one of the progress, the ongoing emergence, of greater complexity and sophistication. As process philosophy rather optimistically sees it, transiency is the price that the world's scheme of things exacts for the ongoing realization of higher-level values.

The processual view of life recognizes the aspect of transiency, giving prominence to such *obiter dicta* as "Carpe diem," "We go around only once," "Life must be lived in the present." But it also recognizes that the present is not all— that for human beings the immediacy of the moment is always conditioned by visions of the future. And here the salient fact is not just "Here today, gone tomorrow" but that we humans always have a stake in a tomorrow that we will not live to see. In this sense, an intelligent creature is amphibious, with a stake at once in both the transitory present and the ever-beckoning future. We enlarge our transitory selves and enrich the quality of our appreciations as we expand our horizons of our concerns and interests.

Plato said in the *Symposium* that what is "in reality new [is also continuous with the old] according to that law of succession by which all mortal things are preserved, not absolutely the same, but by substitution, the old worn-out mortality leaving another new and similar existence behind."[15] Along these lines, processists stress that while we humans live on "borrowed time," we nevertheless have a foothold in eternity. For while *individuals* are transitory, the values and excellences they generally prize and sometimes actualize need not be so. In a processual world no single item is preserved as such, but we can nevertheless have a stake in enduring— though also evolving—values and ideals. True, in a world of process everything short of the whole itself is transitory. But the transiency of process does not destroy value—the beauty of a symphonic performance is not negated by the fact that it has an ending. (Indeed, it would not have the sort of beauty it does if it did not.)

7

Process Logic and Epistemology

SYNOPSIS

(1) Knowledge aims at the truth of things, and this appears to be something inert and changeless, seeing that the mainstream logical theory of the West takes an approach to truth that is committed to its static fixity. (2) However, the idea of truth-value definiteness and stability was already dismissed at the very origin of logic by Aristotle himself. (3) It is a grave mistake to see inquiry as a thing-oriented venture geared to the acquisition of substantive items of information or knowledge: the "true facts." Irrespective of any fixity in its objects, human knowledge as such is something fluid and ever-changing. (4) Not only is the substance of our knowledge (information, facts) subject to change, but so are the very ideas or concepts that function in such contexts. (5) The development and communication of information in a communal setting is in all of its aspects an active and thoroughly processual enterprise.

1. TRUTH AND KNOWLEDGE: THE PROCESSUAL PERSPECTIVE

Epistemology, the theory of knowledge, concerns itself with the ways and means by which we humans attempt to establish the truth of things. But truth as such seems to have a rather hard-edged finality about it. The truth on some matter is, to all appearance, something altogether fixed and stable: once really true, always really true. How does this square with a process-oriented view of things?

"The rose is red." "The rose is blossoming." Unlike Spanish, English (like most other European languages) has no natural way of distinguishing the *is* of description (*ser*) at issue in the former classificatory case from the *is* of activity (*estar*) at work in the latter, activity-indicative one. Yet from a logical point of view the two are substantially different. For better or worse, the mainstream Western tradition of theorizing about logic and language has chosen to focus upon the former issue of stable assertion to the deemphasis of of indicating transitory conditions, thereby validating a bias toward static fixity and inert definiteness.[1] But in taking such an approach to the truth—one that is committed to its stability—the tradition has enmeshed itself in problems. For wherever there is change (activity, process)—as there certainly is throughout the real world—matters stand neither exactly the one way nor exactly the other. The future of affairs parts ways from their present condition in ways that are deeply problematic from the angle of the here-and-now in which our communicative business must be transacted. And so the bias of our language to stable characterizations does not smoothly accommodate a situation where change and its uncertainties come into play. Interestingly, this is something that Aristotle himself, the founding father of logic as practiced in the West, already realized acutely (unlike the preponderant majority of his successors). It is instructive for the theory of process to consider how he proposed to deal with the problem.

Our claims to knowledge are part and parcel of a *praxis*—though, to be sure, it is a cognitive or intellectual praxis that is at stake. The substantiation, maintenance, and diffusion of knowledge are all matters of practice governed by the ground rules and principles of a correlative modus operandi. Process philosophers and pragmatists alike have always stressed the status of knowledge as a process. John Dewey, in particular, dismissed the "spectator theory of knowledge," insisting that the acquisition and management of factual knowledge is always a matter of interacting with our circumambient human and natural environment. We come here to a distinction that has far-reaching implications.

There has been a common but very questionable tendency among philosophers to treat knowledge as something substantial—as a grasp of certain "things" called facts which, if all goes well, have truth as a fixed attribute ("true facts"). And this has been accompanied by the equally problematic tendency to treat inquiry as a thing-oriented project that issues in the acquisition or recognition such substantive items as "pieces of information or knowledge." But this whole perspective is predicated on the grave fallacy of seeing information (knowledge) as a sort of substance, a commodity of sorts. It is clear (and relatively uncontroversial) that inquiring, discovering, formulating, confirming, and communicating knowledge are all epistemic processes. But beyond this there is also the circumstance that the so-called objects at issue—the "facts" being investigated, discerned, transmitted, etc.—are themselves "process-coordinated": They are not things or entities in their own right, but practical resources at our disposal in the content of our cognitive affairs.[2]

The substantialist approach to knowledge is thus deeply problematic. Inquiry is *not* productive of any sort of thinglike commodity. Insofar as successful inquiry is involved in the production of something, what it engenders is not a *substantive* product. Knowledge is not substantial but is inseparably geared toward action in origin and function. The acquisition of information always resides in a capacity to carry on certain processes; it is a matter of being able to carry out certain performances successfully (generally in the line of inquiring processes), and not one of achieving ownership of things of some sort. To see information as a literal *product* (a substance of some sort) is to commit the fallacy of improper reification—of "misplaced concreteness," as Whitehead called it.

It is instructive in this context to contrast three different approaches to the theory of knowledge. First is the theory of *representative* cognition (in the tradition of Descartes with his mind/matter dualism), which sees true thought about factual matters as somehow representing a totally nonmental state of affairs. (This winds up in the bankruptcy of the Kantian thing-in-itself.) Second is the theory of *constructive* cognition, which (in the best idealistic tradition) takes the idealistic line that in true thought we are dealing with mind-engendered constructions—either a theological construction, as with Berkeley, or a naturalistic construction of inquiring individuals or communities, as with Hegel. (This winds up with the artificiality of the various versions of all-out idealism.) The prime remaining possibility is the *causal-commerce* theory of cognition, which sees true thought and its object as simply two phases of the real caught up in a process of mutual interconnection. This approach—favored by processism—of factual knowledge in terms of a harmonious overall manifold of causal commerce in which the "external" order of nature and the "internal" order of physiologico-psychological come into suitable alignment. The traditional representational and constructive theories of cognition are now not so much refined as replaced.

2. Aristotle and Truth-Value Indeterminacy

In the celebrated sea battle discussion of chapter 9 of his On Interpretation (*De interpretatione*), Aristotle set out his well-known thesis maintaining the indeterminate truth status of statements regarding future contingencies.[3] A present claim about a contingent future occurrence, such as the sea battle tomorrow, is—so Aristotle here maintains—neither true or false, but actually *lacks* any such definite truth condition until after the issue is ultimately settled, one way or the other, as an accomplished fact. Before the event, the truth status of statements regarding future contingencies remains suspended in a limbo of indeterminacy: There being as yet no fact of the matter, we confront a bivalence-violating situation in which the future-oriented statements at issue are neither true nor false. We reach here the logically unorthodox situation of having some perfectly meaningful statements be neither true nor false, making their truth status hinge wholly upon subsequent contingent developments in the world's course of change.

And there are other contexts where the same sort of truth-value indeterminacy is called for on Aristotelian principles. For example, something which is coming into being cannot (ex hypothesi) be said to exist as yet.[4] After all, "coming to be (*genesis*) is a passing away if that which is not, and passing away (*phtora*) is a coming to be of what is not" (*De gener. corr.*, 319a28). Nevertheless, at the point of its genesis, a substance is already somehow at hand, since "it" already is doing something—viz., emerging into existence—so that there already is a something to which that coming-into-being can be attributed. We therefore cannot flatly and unqualifiedly deny the thing's existence either. The claim of its existence is thus neither strictly true nor strictly false. Accordingly, the existentially nebulous condition of that which is becoming (or is ceasing to be) at the precise juncture when it is entering into (or is exiting from) actual existence makes it plausible to see truth-value indeterminacy as implicated no less in becoming that in future contingency. Here too, then, we encounter truth-value indeterminacy with "The thing now exists" failing—then and there—to be either definitely true or definitely false. The statement "X exists (at the present moment)," asserted with respect to the time of its genesis, is in this regard on all fours with the statement "A sea battle occurs at time t," asserted with respect to the future. The latter statement acquires a definite truth-value only with the arrival t itself—and contingently on the state of affairs then prevailing. The former statement acquires a definite truth value only with the arrival of X itself, and thereafter changes this status from true to false upon X's passage into nonexistence, with a transitional truth indeterminancy at the moment or juncture of its actual demise. On this perspective, truth-value indeterminacy is implicated no less in coming to be and passing away than it is in the context of situations of future contingency.

Moreover, Aristotle's treatment of Zeno's paradoxes of motion might also be brought upon the stage of consideration in the present context. This is set out in its fullest detail in chapter 9 of Book VI of the *Physics*. Since motion and change are involved in all of these paradoxes in more or less the same way, it will suffice for present purposes to look at one of them. Thus consider the "Flying Arrow" paradox. This roots in the question of just what the flying arrow is doing at a given moment (instant). On the one hand, it cannot be moving, because things do not move at instants—a momentary instant is simply too short a time to admit of a change of position. On the other hand, the arrow cannot be immobile (unmoving, remaining fixed in place) at the instants during its journey.

For if it is immobile at every moment throughout the interval of its supposed flight, then it never moves at all—and thus can accomplish no motion. However, once the prospect of truth-status indeterminacy is accepted, the paradox is readily resolved. For the horns of Zeno's paradox are now evaded in a straightforward way on this basis seeing that the statement "The arrow is right now (at this very instant) flying" is one that cannot appropriately be classed as either true or false for the very reasons set out in formulating the paradox. For the dilemmatic choice between the arrow's actually moving or remaining immobile at a given instant is now averted, seeing that at any particular moment the arrow can neither be truly said to be in motion (since instants admit no movement) nor yet be said to be at rest (i.e., not in motion) since it is, ex hypothesi, flying. The problem that Zeno's arrow paradox poses for the theory of motion falls away with recourse to truth-value indeterminate statements.

The modern process philosopher can thus extract some very useful and instructive lessons from Aristotle's handling of problems of future contingency. For the concept of semantical indeterminacy provides ready made a very effective and serviceable resource not only for Aristotelian metaphysics but for an adequate theory of process. It is clear that any philosophy in which process in its various guises of origination, motion, and change plays a significant role—in short, any adequate metaphysics whatsoever—will face substantial theoretical problems in fitting the comparatively stable and rigidly determinate categories of orthodox logic and semantics to the more fluid and volatile reality that such a metaphysics envisions. It has to confront the sorts of puzzles and paradoxes with which the ancients already grappled in the context of Zeno's puzzles and those at issue with the sorites paradox and its cognates. And, as Aristotle already saw, a logic of truth-value indeterminacy affords a potent and effective instrument for the accommodation of such paradoxes.

The very fact that Aristotle needed to make exceptions within his substance/attribute framework for these issues of change and future contingency bears witness to the comparative advantage of a process-oriented approach in metaphysics.

After all, processes put the position of affairs into an in-between condition that is neither here nor there—a condition where it is never altogether appropriate to say simply "Yes" but rather only "Yes-but." The fluidity of natural process (its "analog" nature and its kinship to the continuities captured by differential equations and the mathematics of infinitesimals) is out of alignment with the rigidities of everyday language (with its "digital," yes-or-no, on-or-off nature). Recourse to a grey region of truth-status indeterminacy is accordingly a useful mediating device for handling those aspects of the world's modus operandi that process philosophy is concerned to emphasize. So useful, indeed, is this device that process philosophers would have had to devise it themselves had Aristotle not already done so for them.

3. The Processual Nature of Knowledge and the Cognitive Inexhaustibility of Things

The processual nature of knowledge reflects the fact that our thought about the real things of this world presses outward beyond the limit of any restrictive boundaries. From finitely many axioms reason can generate a potential infinity of theorems; from finitely many words thought can exfoliate a potential infinity of sentences; from finite data reflection can extract a potential infinity of items of information. Even with a world of finitely many objects, the process of gaining information about these objects can, in principle, go on unendingly. One can inquire about their features, the features of these features, and so on; or, again, one can consider their relations, the relations among those relations, and so on. Thought—abstraction, reflection, analysis—is an inherently ampliative process. As in physical reflection, where mirror images can reflect one another indefinitely, so mental reflection can go on and on. Given a start, however modest, thought can advance ad indefinitum into new conceptual domains.

The number of true descriptive remarks that can be made about any actual physical object is always potentially inexhaustible. For example, take a stone. Consider its physical features: its shape, surface texture, chemistry, and so forth. And then consider its causal background: its genesis and subsequent history. Then consider its functional aspects as relevant to its uses by the stonemason, the architect, the landscape decorator, and so on. There is, in principle, no theoretical limit to the different lines of consideration available to yield descriptive truths about any real thing whatever. Our knowledge of the real is in principle inexhaustible. The circumstance of its starting out from a finite basis does not mean that it need ever run out of impetus (as the example of Shakespearean scholarship seems to illustrate).

Moreover, the prospect of transiency can never be eliminated in this cognitive domain. Where the real things of the world are concerned, not only do we expect to learn more about them in the course of scientific inquiry, but *we expect to have to change our minds about their nature and modes of comportment.* Be the items at issue elm trees or volcanoes or quarks, we have every expectation that, in the course of future scientific progress, people will—in the times of ample experience—come to think about their origin and their properties differently from the way we do at this juncture. Knowledge is far more like a process than a thing.

The very concepts at issue with "experience" and "manifestation" are such that we can only ever *experience* those features of a real thing that it actually *manifests*. But real things always have more experientially manifestable properties than they can ever actually manifest in experience. The experienced portion of a thing is just the part of the iceberg that shows above water. All real things are necessarily thought of as having hidden depths that extend beyond the limits not only of experience but also of experientiability. To say of something that it is an apple or a stone or a tree is to become committed to claims about it that go beyond the data we have—and even beyond those that we can in the nature of things ever actually acquire. The meaning inherent in the assertoric commitments of our factual statements is never exhausted by its verification. Real things are cognitively opaque—we cannot see to the bottom of them. Our knowledge of such things can thus become more extensive without thereby becoming more complete.

This cognitive opacity of real things means that we are not—and will never be—in a position to evade or abolish the contrast between "things as we think think them to be" and "things as they actually and truly are." Their susceptibility to ever more elaborate detail and to changes of mind regarding this further detail is built into our very conception of real things. To be real is to be something regarding which we can always, in principle, acquire further new information, which may not only supplement but even correct that which has previously been acquired. This view of the situation is bolstered rather than impeded once we abandon the naive cumulativist/preservationist view of knowledge acquisition for the view that new discoveries need not augment but can displace old ones. With further inquiry, we may come to recognize the error of our earlier ways of thinking about the things at issue. We realize that people will come to think differently about things from the way we do—even when thoroughly familiar things are at issue—recognizing that scientific progress generally entails fundamental changes of mind about how things work in the world.

And much the same story holds when our concern is not with knowledge of *individual* things but with *types* of such things. To say that something is copper or magnetic is to say more than that it has the properties we think copper or magnetic things have, and to say more than that it meets our test conditions for being copper or being magnetic. It is to say that this thing truly and definitively *is* copper or magnetic—come what may. And this is an issue regarding which we are prepared at least to contemplate the prospect that we have got it wrong.

In view of the cognitive opacity of the real, we always do well to refrain from pretending to a cognitive monopoly or cognitive finality. This recognition of incomplete information is inherent in the very nature of our conception of a "real thing." It is a crucial facet of our epistemic stance toward the real world to recognize that every bit of it has features lying beyond our present cognitive reach—at *any* "present" whatsoever.

We are led back in this connection to the thesis of the great idealist philosophers (Spinoza, Hegel, Bradley, Royce) that actual human knowledge inevitably falls short of "perfected science" (the Idea, the Absolute) and must be presumed deficient both in its completeness and its correctness. And our deliberations about our cognitive limitedness have a further deeply idealistic aspect, for the fundamental fact of the literally *unending* cognitive depth of real things—their bottomless cognitive depth—is not actually a *discovery* that we make about them. It is not something that we learn about things in the course of experiential interaction with the real. Instead, it reflects an aspect of our very conception of what it is to be "real"; for it is an integral feature of our conception of the real that the actual nature of the world's furnishings outruns our current knowledge of them. Our knowledge of fact is always in flux. It is not a thing, a definite corpus, but an ever-changing and ever-growing manifold of process.[5]

4. PROCESS AND EXPERIENCE

Idea formation is a salient and characteristic capacity of intelligent beings, and *experience*—that is to say, the interaction between minds and nature—is the pivotal mode of process here. The empiricists were right at any rate in this: that all our ideas have a basis in experience. But they were wrong in thinking that this experience had to be sensory rather than more broadly speaking intellectual. As Kant stressed, empiricists neglected the crucial fact that all our experience is ideational (or conceptual) in nature. To be sure, our experience is *intentional*, it is always *of* something and is accordingly object oriented. But, of course, the object at issue need not be something *substantive* and thinglike. Processes as such also count. In fact, they are central. To be experienced is to feature in an encounter that has a certain adjectival cast; the intentionality of an experience—its being an experience of an X—resides in the manner and make-up of its unfolding: that the proceeding at issue proceeds Xly.

This aspect of the cognitive enterprise is brought to the fore in the relationship between observation and process that was emphasized by A. P. Ushenko in his *Power and Events*. What we actually experience, he maintained, is not a matter of the sense data of earlier perception theorists, emplaced in a static copresence like letters to a printed page. We experience the powers of things—not just the engine but its throbbings, not just the flames but their radiating warmth, not just the redness of Smith's face but his anger. We observe not just things but their activities and operations. And this brings their process—their causal efficacy—into the orbit of experience. Human observation is a commerce with the world's processes, a dynamic encounter that is not just a matter of a noting of its fixed features.

At any given temporal juncture, language is something limited and finite. But reality outruns any such limitation. Even with such familiar things as birds, trees, and clouds, we are involved in a constant reconceptualization in the course of progress in genetics, evolutionary theory, and thermodynamics. Our conceptions of things always present a moving rather than a fixed object of scrutiny, and this historical dimension must also be reckoned with.

Not only is the substance of our knowledge (information, facts) deeply processual, but so are the very ideas that are at work here which, after all, themselves operate processually defined states of the cognitive art. Any adequate theory of inquiry must recognize that the ongoing process of information acquisition at issue in science is a process of *conceptual* innovation, which always leaves certain facts about things wholly outside the cognitive range of the inquirers of any particular period. Caesar did not know (and in the then-extant state of the cognitive art could not have known) that his sword contained tungsten and carbon. There will always be facts about a thing that we do not know because we cannot even conceive of them in the prevailing conceptual order of things. To grasp such a fact means taking a perspective of consideration that we as yet simply do not have, since the state of knowledge (or purported knowledge) has not reached a point at which such a consideration is feasible.

For present purposes, the crucial consideration is that our knowledge of reality itself has an operational/practical and thus processual dimension. One of the most significant and characteristic kinds of know-how is the knowledge of how to operate at the level of theory—how to conjure with theoretical knowledge-that over the range from obtaining it to using and conveying it. Here we come to the whole domain of securing, recording, communicating, and processing information. Achieving any sort of knowledge-that is itself one of the most extensive and significant forms of praxis in which our species is involved. And, of course, praxis is by its very nature something processual. Any adequate worldview must recognize that the ongoing progress of scientific inquiry is a process of conceptual innovation that always leaves various facts about the things of this world wholly outside the cognitive range of the inquirers of any particular period. Ideas cannot be grasped before their time—before the developmental unfolding of the beliefs and notions that alone can provide an intellectual entryway into their domain. The novelty that arises with the emergence of new cognitive processes is crucial both to the nature and to the availability of our ideas. This dynamics of ideas strikingly marks the processual aspect of epistemology. Throughout the cognitive enterprise we are confronted with an ever-changing state of the art. Knowledge is not a thing, let alone a commodity of a fixed and stable make-up; it is irremediably processual in nature, affected as deeply by the fluid nature of reality as anything else.

5. PROCESS AND COMMUNICATION

And this processuality holds not just for the development and comprehension of knowledge but for its communication as well. In general, processes have three phases or stages:

> initiating precursors → the process itself →
> resultant successors.

Processes standardly exhibit such a pattern of sequential order, be it a temporal or a conceptual order that is at issue. And in the case of specifically communicative processes we have

> informative inputs → the communication itself →
> informative outputs.

In effect, these three stages reflect the question of (i) symbol-use conditions, (ii) the symbolic process itself, and (iii) symbol-use results (information transfer).[6] From this standpoint, the enterprise of communication is also to be regarded in a thoroughly processual perspective. And this is only appropriate. For communication is ill served by being depicted as a commerce in "things" as per the misleading reifications of symbols, messages, and meanings. These are no more than suppositional abstractions, useful, perhaps, as shorthand devices for presenting considerations which themselves are of a very different status—not "things" of some sort but processes at work in the ideational transactions of informative thought.

This view of communication as a process of information transmission across the diversity of persons and times is characteristic of a process epistemology which sees this sort of convenience in information not as a matter of manipulating with ideational objects (beliefs, messages, or the like) but rather as one of conveying information with a view to its use by oneself and others within a characteristic range of processual operations.[7] After all, the communication of information that is indispensably necessary to the acquisition and confirmation of knowledge in a communal setting is clearly also a thoroughly processual enterprise. And, moreover, the interpretation of communicated symbols the transformation of physical signals into informative messages is itself inevitably a process, one to which the recipient also has to make an active contribution.

And this circumstance has larger implications. For process philosophers, the most fundamental and pervasive factor of reality is its instability—its being a flux. And this circumstance encompasses knowledge itself. It too is in a constant state of flux. And this means that reality cannot be adequately (i.e., more than approximately) represented and conveyed by the relatively fixed and discrete mechanisms of language and its concepts. Symbolic representation of purported fact is virtually always unfaithful to reality—our descriptive formulations are not to be taken too literally. To some extent they are generally figurative—mere likenesses. In the final analysis, our attempts to characterize the world's arrangements by linguistic means must be acknowledged as almost inevitably being in some degree metaphorical.

As far as the process philosopher is concerned, Plato's story of the cave stood matters on their head. For it is not that reality is something static and immune from alteration (along the lines of Plato's "realm of Ideas") while our imperfect human conceptions are fluctuating and moveable, but, rather, it is the other way round: Our conceptions are too inflexible and inert to accommodate an ever-changing reality. Yet the net effect is the same either way: Our human conceptual thinking always involves some distortion of fact, some unfaithfulness to reality. And here the role of metaphor is crucial. At bottom, linguistic communication as we know it builds on a comparatively small basis of practically geared literal language use. But this is infinitely enriched and amplified by metaphorical flights—processes of assimilation that extend its communicative resources into every direction. (And note that this very sentence itself manifests the very process at issue in its use of "implement," "flight," and "extend in a direction.") The metaphorical nature of linguistic communication is yet another aspect of the many-sidedly processual nature of human cognition.[8]

From the process standpoint, then, it emerges that the purposes of an adequate understanding of knowledge acquisition and management are ill served by a problematic reification of the elements of knowledge into thought-things. Human knowledge is geared to activity; its terms of reference are given by verbs like asserting, questioning, understanding, communicating, and so forth. From the epistemological and logical point of view, those abstract items at issue in communication—meanings, data, and the rest—are convenient fictions devised to describe, compare, and contrast the fundamentally processual phenomena of acquiring, transmitting, storing, and utilizing information. To make substancelike "things" of cognitive and communicative matters is once again to commit Whitehead's fallacy of misplaced concreteness. The development, employment, and communication of information in a communal setting is in all of its aspects an active and thoroughly processual enterprise.

And, as we shall now see, this circumstance is nowhere more clearly manifest than in natural science.

8

A Processual View of Scientific Inquiry

SYNOPSIS

(1) The processual nature of knowledge is nowhere more clearly manifest than in our scientific knowledge. Science, properly understood, is not a body of theses or theories, but a process—an ongoing venture in inquiry whose products are ever changing. (2) We cannot predict the future of science: In this domain the present is unable to speak for the future. (3) Scientific progress is driven by technological progress—a circumstance that will, in the end, spell its incompleteness since there is always, in principle, more to be done in this direction. Not only the methods and procedures but also the products of scientific inquiry are inherently processual.

1. INQUIRY AS A PRODUCTIVE PROCESS: THE EXAMPLE OF SCIENCE

The processual nature of knowledge becomes vividly apparent through the historical progress of "scientific knowledge" that has been recognized since classical antiquity.[1] The history of science and human inquiry in all its forms clearly shows that facts, theories, concepts, and methods are not entities with a fixed and stable nature but process-geared eventuations that changeably reflect the cognitive state of the art of a place, time, and cultural modus operandi. What appear as the timeless truths of one era are merely transitory beliefs from the vantage point of another. Human cognition is something that actively develops, and with this development we have not only change but the emergence of a novelty that always divides the present from what has gone before.

The crux of process epistemology lies in its (clearly right-minded) insistence on seeing the enterprise of rational inquiry—be it in natural science or elsewhere—as being a process. It is concerned not with the embodiment of information and knowledge as a physical artifact along the lines of a book or blueprint or library catalog but with the living and changing dynamics of such materials. In particular, we have to recognize that the sort of rational inquiry at issue in the scientific enterprise is something which is, from the angle of its products—theories, theses, explanations, and so forth—something that is ever transitory and provisional, ever constrained to give up old claims in the light of new evidence and enhanced information. And this, all too clearly, makes it natural to regard science as a process rather than as a certain product. It focuses upon living cognitive activity—the unfolding procedures (techniques, methods) that people use to discover, systematize, and transmit information. On this basis, active inquiry, information processing, and communication come to be seen as the key components of the scientific venture as a processual enterprise.

Such a perspective indicates that science is not a "body of knowledge"—an aggregate of information, stably stored away in books and journals and computer tapes but rather an activity, an enterprise, a discipline—a living endeavor of search and research, of inquiry, of ventures in the resolution of questions. Scientific knowledge is nothing fixed and given, but rather is encompassed in a set of practices through which the scientific community actively pursues the business of problem resolution. And the scientific status of a thesis is a matter not of what it says but of how it actively figures in the scientific process. Thus, as the process approach views the matter, science is as science does—that is, as scientists actively work with it.

The equilibrium achieved by natural science at any given stage of its development is invariably an unstable one. The history of science shows all to clearly that many of our scientific theories about the workings of nature have a finite lifespan. They come to be modified or replaced in the light of further investigation effected through improved techniques of experimentation, more powerful means of observation and detection, superior procedures for data processing, and the like. The "state of the art" of natural science is a human artifact that, like all other human creations, falls subject to the ravages of time. We learn by empirical inquiry about empirical inquiry, and one of the key things we learn is that at no actual stage does science yield a final and unchanging result. All the experience we can muster indicates that there is no justification for regarding our present-day science as more than an inherently imperfect stage within an ongoing development. The landscape of science is ever changing. As fallibilists since C. S. Peirce's day have insisted, we must acknowledge an inability to attain definitive truth in scientific matters.

But why do theories fail? What aspect of reality accounts for this state of affairs? In a way, the answer lies in the fact that scientific theories are human products, and in the course of time all human contrivances fail. All human artifacts and constructions are fragile, transitory, and destined ultimately to collapse. Any human creation—be it a house, a dam, or a knowledge-claim—is designed to function under certain known (or surmised) conditions. But the processes of change that come with time always bring new, unforeseen and unforeseeable circumstances to the fore. The best-laid productions of mice and men come to grief under the impact of the world's volatile contingencies.[2] And this impermanence— this vulnerability to the pervasive dominion of chaos over the things of this world—holds just as much for our intellectual constructions as for our physical structures. It thereby predestines the ultimate failure of even our best explanatory efforts.

Another aspect of the matter lies in the nature of scientific inquiry itself. Our scientific explanations are based on theories, and almost inevitably our scientific theories (like every other human construction) will ultimately encounter destabilizing conditions. A scientific theory is a structure built to house, and attuned to the needs of, a certain body of experiences—fitted to the conditions of observation and information processing of a particular technological state of the art. As these conditions change, stresses and strains develop which destabilize the theory-structure and lead to its eventual collapse. Changed social conditions destabilize social systems. Changed physical conditions destabilize structures. Changed experiential (i.e., experimental and observational) conditions—changed scientific technology, if you will—destabilize scientific theories. Natural science is not only imperfect but imperfectible.[3] And this fact has profound implications both for the predictions that we make through science and for those that we can make about it.

2. Difficulties in Predicting Future Science: In Natural Science, the Present Cannot Speak for the Future

The future of science is an enigma. Innovation is the very name of the game. Not only do the theses and themes of science change but so do the very questions. Of course, once a body of science comes to be seen as something settled and firmly in hand, many issues become routine. Various problems become mere reference questions—a matter of locating an answer within the body of preestablished, already available information that somewhere contains it. (The *mere* here is, to be sure, misleading in downplaying the formidable challenges that can arise in looking for needles in large haystacks.) However, in pioneering science we face a very different situation. People may well wonder what the cause of *X* is—what causes cancer, say, or what produces the attraction of the lodestone for iron—in circumstances where the concepts needed to develop a workable answer are entirely beyond their grasp.

Innovation is the order of the day in science, and surprises are unavoidable. Commenting shortly after the publication of Frederick Soddy's speculations about atomic bombs in his 1930 book *Science and Life*,[4] Robert A. Millikan, a Nobel laureate in physics, wrote that "the new evidence born of further scientific study is to the effect that it is highly improbable that there is any appreciable amount of available subatomic energy to tap."[5] In science forecasting, the record of even the most qualified practitioner is poor. For people may well not even be able to conceive the explanatory mechanisms of which future science will make routine use. As one sagacious observer noted over a century ago:

> There is no necessity for supposing that the true explanation must be one which, with only our present experience, *we could* imagine. Among the natural agents with which we are acquainted, the vibrations of an elastic fluid may be the only one whose laws bear a close resemblance to those of light; but we cannot tell that there does not exist an unknown cause, other than an elastic ether diffused through space, yet producing effects identical in some respects with those which would result from the undulations of such an ether. To assume that no such cause can exist, appears to me an extreme case of assumption without evidence.[6]

Since we cannot predict the answers to the presently open questions of natural science, we also cannot predict its future questions, seeing that these are generally engendered by the answers to those we have on hand. Most of the questions with which present-day science grapples could not even have been raised in the state of the art that prevailed a generation ago.

In scientific inquiry as in other areas of human affairs, major upheavals can come about fortuitously, in a manner that is sudden, unanticipated, and often unwelcome. Major breakthroughs often result from research projects that have very different ends in view. Louis Pasteur's discovery of the protective efficacy of inoculation with weakened disease strains affords a striking example. While studying chicken cholera, Pasteur accidentally inoculated a group of chickens with a weak culture. The chickens became ill but, instead of dying, recovered. Pasteur later reinoculated these chickens with fresh culture—one strong enough to kill an ordinary chicken. To Pasteur's surprise, the chickens remained healthy. Pasteur then shifted his attention to this interesting phenomenon, and a productive new line of investigation opened up. In empirical inquiry, we generally cannot tell in advance what further questions will be engendered by our endeavors to answer those on hand. New scientific questions arise from answers we give to previous ones, and thus the issues of future science simply lie beyond our present horizons.

Not being able to foresee new questions, we certainly cannot foresee new answers. We know—or at any rate can safely predict—*that* future science will make major discoveries (both theoretical and observational/phenomenological) in the next century, but we cannot say *what* they are and *how* they will be made (since otherwise we could proceed to make them here and now). We could not possibly predict now the substantive content of our future scientific, since doing so would be to transform them into present discoveries which, by hypothesis, they just are not.[7] In cognitive forecasting it is the errors of omission—our blind spots, as it were—that present the most serious threat. For the fact is that we cannot substantially anticipate the evolution of knowledge. Given past experience, we can feel reasonably secure when we say that science will resolve various problems in the future; But how it will do so is bound to be a mystery.[8] With respect to the major substantive issues of future natural science, we must be prepared for the unexpected. Radical change is inescapable.

Not only can one never claim with confidence that the science of tomorrow will not resolve the issues that the science of today sees as intractable, but one can never be sure that the science of tomorrow will not endorse principles that the science of today rejects. This is why it is always risky to speak of this or that explanatory resource (action at a distance, stochastic processes, mesmerism, etc.) as inherently unscientific. Even if X lies outside the range of science as we nowadays construe it, it by no means follows that X lies outside science as such. We must recognize the commonplace phenomenon that the science of the day almost always manages to do what the science of an earlier day deemed infeasible to the point of absurdity (split the atom, abolish parity, etc.). With natural science, the substance of the future inevitably lies beyond our present grasp. An innovative process of the sort at issue here is unavoidably imponderable. The development of science is not only a process, but one ever-destined to bring surprises.

3. SCIENTIFIC PROGRESS IS DRIVEN BY TECHNOLOGICAL ESCALATION

The fundamentally processive and progressive nature of natural science can be regarded from another point of view. In natural science, the driving force of innovation is provided by technology, for observation and experimentation both need to be technologically mediated. Here progress is possible only where we can do more than before, thanks to a more powerful technology. This requirement for technological progress to advance scientific knowledge has far-reaching implications for the nature of the enterprise. Natural science is fundamentally empirical, and its advance is critically dependent not on human ingenuity alone but also on the monitoring observations to which we can gain access only through interactions with nature. The days are long past when useful scientific data can be had by unaided sensory observation of the ordinary course of nature. Artifice has become an indispensable route to the acquisition and processing of scientifically useful data. The sorts of data on which scientific discovery nowadays depends can be generated only by means of a technology on which we must make ever greater demands. As one acute observer has rightly remarked, "Most critical experiments [in physics] planned today, if they had to be constrained within the technology of even ten years ago, would be seriously compromised."[9] Observational, experimental, and information-processing technology is driven on an endless quest for substantial (order-of-magnitude) improvements in performance with regard to such information-providing parameters as measurement exactness, data-processing volume, detection sensitivity, high voltages, and high or low temperatures. Throughout the natural sciences, technological progress is a crucial requisite for cognitive progress.

In developing natural science, we humans began by exploring the world in our own locality—not just our spatial neighborhood but our parametric neighborhood in the space of physical variables such as temperature, pressure, and electrical charge. Near the "home base" of the parametric state of things prevailing in our accustomed natural environment, we can—thanks to the evolutionary heritage of our sensory and cognitive apparatus—operate with relative ease and freedom by scanning nature with the unassisted senses for data regarding its modes of operation. But in due course we accomplish everything that can be managed by these unsophisticated means. To do more, we have to extend our probes into nature more deeply, deploying increasing technical sophistication and power to achieve more and more demanding levels of interactive capability. We have to move even further away from our evolutionary home base in nature toward increasingly remote frontiers. From the anthropocentric standpoint of our local region of parameter space, we have, over time, journeyed ever more distantly outward to explore nature's various parametric dimensions, in the manner of a prospector, searching for cognitively significant phenomena.

The appropriate picture is not, of course, one of geographical exploration but one of the physical exploration—and subsequent theoretical systematization—of phenomena distributed over the parametric space of the physical quantities spreading out all about us. This analogy of exploration provides for a conception of scientific research as a prospecting search for the new phenomena needed for significant new scientific findings. As the range of telescopes, the energy of particle accelerators, the effectiveness of low-temperature instrumentation, the potency of pressurization equipment, the power of vacuum-creating contrivances, and the accuracy of measurement apparatus increases—that is, as our capacity to move about in the parametric space of the physical world is enhanced—new phenomena come into view. The key to the great progress of contemporary physics lies in the enormous strides which an ever more sophisticated scientific technology enables us to make by enlarging the empirical basis of our knowledge of natural processes.[10]

The enormous power, sensitivity, and complexity deployed in present-day experimental science have not been sought for their own sake but rather because the research frontier has moved on into an area where this sophistication is the indispensable requisite of ongoing progress. In science, as in war, the battles of the present cannot be fought effectively with the armaments of the past. Without the innovation processes that engender an ever-developing technology, scientific progress would soon grind to a halt. The discoveries of today cannot be made with yesterday's equipment and techniques. To conduct new experiments, to secure new observations, and to detect new phenomena, an ever more powerful investigative technology is needed. Scientific progress depends crucially and unavoidably on our technical capability to penetrate into the increasingly distant—and increasingly difficult—reaches of the spectrum of physical parameters, to explore and to explain the ever more remote phenomena encountered there. As an army marches on its stomach, so science advances on its technology.

Progress in natural science is a matter of dialogue or debate between theoreticians and experimentalists. The experimentalists probe nature to see its reactions, to seek out new phenomena and make them accessible to observation. The theoreticians, for their part, take the resultant data and weave a theoretical fabric about them. Seeking to devise a framework of rational understanding, they construct their explanatory models to accommodate the findings that the experimentalists put at their disposal. But once the theoreticians have had their say, the ball returns to the experimentalists' court. Employing new, ever more powerful means for probing nature, they bring new phenomena to view, new data for accommodation. Precisely because these data are new and inherently unpredictable, they often fail to fit the old theories. Theory extrapolations from the old data could not encompass them; the old theories do not accommodate them. The technologically mediated entry into new regions of parameter space constantly destabilizes the attained equilibrium between data and theory. At this stage, the ball reenters the theoreticians' court. New theories must be devised to accommodate the new, nonconforming data. And so the theoreticians set about weaving a new theoretical structure to accommodate the new data. They endeavor to create, once more, an equilibrium between theory and data. And then the ball returns to the experimentalists' court, and the whole process starts over again with its demand for new and more powerful technological capacity.

In natural science, then, we are embarked on a potentially limitless project of improving the range of effective experimental intervention, because only by operating under new and heretofore inaccessible conditions of observational or experimental systematization—attaining extreme temperature, pressure, particle velocity, field strength, and so on—can we realize those circumstances that enable us to put our hypotheses and theories to the test. We thus arrive at the phenomenon of *technological escalation in natural science*. The need for new data forces us to look further and further from man's familiar home base in the parametric space of nature. Thus, while scientific progress is in principle always possible—there being no absolute or intrinsic limits to significant scientific discovery—the realization of this ongoing prospect demands a continual enhancement in the technological state of the art of data extraction or exploitation.

However, our exploration of physical-parameter space is inevitably incomplete. We can never exhaust the whole of these parametric ranges of temperature, pressure, particle velocity, and the like because of physical resistance as one moves toward the extremes. And so we inevitably face the (very real) prospect that the regularity structure of the as-yet-inaccessible cases generally does not conform to the patterns of regularity prevailing in the currently accessible cases. In general, new data just do not accommodate themselves to old theories. (Newtonian calculations, for example, worked marvelously for predicting solar-system phenomenology—eclipses, planetary conjunctions, and the rest—but this did not mean that classical physics was free of any need for fundamental revision.) At every stage of investigative sophistication, we seem to confront a different order or aspect of things. What we find in investigating nature must always, in some degree, reflect the character of our technology of observation, since what we are able to detect in nature is always something that depends on the mechanisms by which we search. And no matter how much we broaden that limited range of currently accessible cases, we can achieve no assurance (or even probability) that a theory corpus that smoothly accommodates the whole range of currently achievable outcomes will hold across the board. The prospect of future change—that is, improvement—can never be confidently foreclosed. But its realization becomes continually more difficult and imposes increasingly greater practical demands.

Ultimately, there will then always be interactions with nature on a scale whose realization requires the deployment of greater resources than we have heretofore expended. But humanity's material resources are limited. And these limits inexorably circumscribe our experiential access to the real world. And when there are interactions to which we have no access, we must presume phenomena that we cannot discern. It would be very odd indeed if nature were to confine the distribution of scientifically significant phenomena to those ranges that happen to lie conveniently within our reach—a condition counterindicated by the whole course of our prior experience.

Given the limitations of our access to nature's phenomena, we must come to terms with the fact that we cannot realistically expect that our science will ever, at any given stage of its development, be in a position to afford us more than a partial and incomplete account of nature. It will never attain the stabilization of a formal completion. For the achievement of cognitive control over nature requires not only intellectual instrumentalities (concepts, ideas, theories, knowledge) but also, and no less importantly, the deployment of physical ones (technology and power). And since the physical resources at our disposal are restricted and finite, it follows that our capacity to effect control is bound to remain imperfect and incomplete, with much in the realm of the doable always remaining undone. We shall never be able to travel down this route as far as we might like to go.

Accordingly, while we can confidently anticipate that our science will undergo ongoing improvement, we cannot expect it ever to attain perfection. There is no reason to think that we ever will, or, indeed, can, reach the end of the road here. Every successive level of technical capability has its inherent limitations, the overcoming of which calls for achieving yet another, more sophisticated, level of the technological state of the art. The intensity of pressure and temperature can in principle always be increased, our low-temperature experiments brought closer to the speed of light, vacua made more and more perfect, and so on. There is no achievable end of the line here; there is always more to be done. And experience teaches that every enhancement of physical mastery brings new phenomena to view, providing an enhanced capability to test yet further hypotheses and to discriminate between new alternative theories to enhance our knowledge of nature.

Progress without new data is, of course, possible in various fields of scholarship and inquiry. The example of pure mathematics, for instance, shows that discoveries can be made in an area of inquiry that operates without empirical data. But this hardly represents a feasible prospect for natural science. It is exactly the explicit dependency on additional data—the empirical aspect of the discipline—that sets natural science apart not only from the formal sciences (logic and mathematics), but also from the hermeneutic ones which (like the humanities) address themselves ceaselessly to the imaginative reinterpretation and re-reinterpretation of old data from novel conceptual perspectives.

Limitations of physical capacity and capability accordingly spell cognitive limitations for empirical science. Where there are inaccessible phenomena there must be cognitive inadequacy as well. To this extent, at any rate, the empiricists were surely right. Only the most fanatical rationalist could uphold the capacity of sheer intellect to compensate for lack of data. The existence of unobserved phenomena means that our theoretical systematizations may well be (and presumably are) incomplete. Insofar as various phenomena are not just undetected but in the very nature of the case inaccessible (even if only for the merely economic reasons suggested above), our theoretical knowledge of nature must be presumed imperfect and incomplete.

And there is something still deeper at work here. Any law of nature is potentially a member of a wider family of laws which will itself exhibit some lawful characteristics and thus be subject to synthesis under still "higher" laws. We thus move from laws governing phenomena (first-order laws) to laws governing such laws (second-order laws) and so on, ascending to new levels of sophistication and comparative complexity as we move along. No matter what law may be at issue, we can ask questions about it that demand an answer in lawful terms. Given such an unending exfoliation of law levels, new metadisciplines can in theory always spring up to relate old disciplines. A fundamental principle is at work here. Since laws take the hypothetical form "If such-and-such possibilities were realized, such-and-such results would ensue," the finitude of the manifold of actuality does not entail the finitude of the diversity of laws. Laws, being hypothetical by nature of their conditional, if–then nature, belong to the domain of possibility, and this domain is not necessarily finitized by the finitude of the actual.[11] The potential for law-novelty in nature is unending.

It is clear that such an infinite proliferation of laws would also serve to block any prospect of completing science. There is thus no need to suppose that the *physical* complexity of nature is unlimited in order for nature to have an unlimited *cognitive* depth. After all, the prime task of science lies in discovering the laws of nature, and the ongoing law complexity of nature suffices for our present purposes of providing for potentially endless discovery.

Fundamental features inherent in the structure of man's interactive inquiry into the ways of the world accordingly conspire to preclude the stabilization—let alone the definitive completion—of the processes at issue in our development of the scientific knowledge of nature, a circumstance that assures for natural science the status of an ongoing process. For not only the procedures but also the products of scientific inquiry are inherently processual, subject to the process-characteristic phases of initiation, development, and decline. The world as science teaches us to see it—is both pervasively variable to our perspectual sight and itself in process of unending development.[12]

9

Process Theology

SYNOPSIS

(1) Process theology, with its abandonment of classical substantialism, puts our understanding of God onto a more straightened, less convoluted path. (2) It accomplishes this by viewing God as an active participant in the world's processual commerce—though, of course, without thereby endowing God with a physical *nature. (3) God's active participation in the world involves processes of many sorts—productive, cognitive, and affective. This participative involvement of the divine in the world's affairs does not, however, preclude human free agency. (4) Process theology is not somehow rooted in science as a doctrine that functions in the explanation of nature's features. The service it renders to understanding does not lie in the order of* explanation *but rather in the order of* appreciation—*in enabling us to apprehend more correctly and clearly the grounds and implications of the fact that the world's arrangements can have worth and value.*

1. GOD: SUBSTANCE OR PROCESS?

We now turn to a very different theme, namely process theology.[1]

To be sure, not all process philosophers are theists—far from it. Process philosophizing has both a theist and a naturalistic wing. The theists see God as a major player in the realm of cosmic process, accounting for the world's order and intelligibility, its creative dynamism, and its teleological normativity. Naturalistic processists, by contrast, see such cosmic macroassets explicable in a nature-immanent way, and view the world as a self-sufficient and self-managing system.[2] The organismic and evolutionary tendencies of process thought offer useful resources to the latter position. But as this chapter will show, the process approach also provides theists with some potent conceptual and theoretical resources.

The neo-Platonic sympathies of the Church Fathers impelled Christian theology to adopt Greek philosophy's stance that in order to see God as existent we must conceive of him as a being, a *substance* of some sort. But, to the enthusiasm of philosophers and the vexation of theologians, this opened up a host of theoretical difficulties. Consider, for example, the following line of reflection: (1) On the traditional conception of the matter, a substance must always originate through the causality of substances. *Q*: So whence God? *A*: He is internally necessitated and free from any and all external causation. (2) Substances standardly have contingent properties. *Q*: Does God? *A*: No, he is in all respects (self-) necessitated. (3) Substances standardly have spatio-temporal emplacement within the world's causal order. *Q*: Does God? *A*: No, he, unlike standard substances, exists altogether outside space and time. And so on. No sooner had Western theology made God a substance in order to satisfy its ontological commitment to the predilections of Greek philosophy than it has to break all of the rules for substances and take away with one hand what it seemed to give with the other. If God is to be viewed as a substance, then this will clearly have to be a very nonstandard sort of substance that is at issue—so nonstandard that one begins to wonder about substantialism's relevancy.

Against this background, it is not surprising that process philosophy, with its characteristic abandonment of classical substantialism, comes to be in a position to put matters on a straighter, less convoluted path. The difficulties of a substance theology offer an open invitation to a process approach in this domain.

2. THE PROCESS VIEW OF GOD

The God of scholastic Christian theology, like the deity of Aristotle on whose model this conception was in part based, is located outside of time—entirely external to the realm of change and process. By contrast, process theologians, however much they may disagree on other matters, take the radical (but surely not heretical) step of according God an active role also *within* the natural world's spatiotemporal frame. They envision a foothold for God also within the overall processual order of the reality that is supposed to be his creation. After all, active participation in the world's processual commerce need not make God into a physical or material object. (While the world indeed contains various physical processes such as the evolution of galaxies, it also contains immaterial processes such as the diffusion of knowledge or the emergence of order.)

For process theology, then, God does not constitute part of the world's matrix of physical processes but nevertheless, in some fashion or other, *participates* in it. Clearly, no ready analogy-model for this mode of participation (spectator, witness, judge, etc.) can begin to do full justice to the situation. But what matters first and foremost from the angle of process theology is *the fact that* God and his world are processually interconnected; the issue of *the manner how* is something secondary that can be left open for further reflection. So conceived, God is not exactly *of* the world of physical reality, but does indeed participate *in* it processually—everywhere touching, affecting, and informing its operations. Thus, while not emplaced in the world, the processists' God is nevertheless bound up with it in an experiential process of interaction with it. In general, process theists do not believe that God actually controls the world. The process God makes an impact persuasively, influencing but never unilaterally imposing the world's process.

Process theology accordingly invites us to think of God's relationship to the world in terms of a process of influence like "the spread of Greek learning in medieval Islam." Greek learning did not become literally *internal* to the Islamic world, but exerted a substantial and extensive influence upon and within it. Analogously, God is not of the world but exerts and extends an all-pervasive influence upon and within it. After all, processes need not themselves be spatial to have an impact upon things in space (think of a price inflation on the economy of a country.) The idea of process provides a category for conceptualizing God's relation to the world that averts many of the difficulties and perplexities of the traditional substance paradigm.

Even apart from process philosophy, various influential theologians have in recent years urged the necessity and desirability of seeing God not through the lens of unchanging stability but with reference to movement, change, development, and process.[3] But the process theorists among theologians want to go beyond this. For them, God is not only to be related to the world's processes in a productive manner, but must himself be regarded in terms of process—as encompassing processuality as a salient aspect of the divine nature.

To be sure, process theologians differ among themselves in various matters of emphasis. Whitehead sees God in cosmological terms as an "actual occasion" functioning within nature, reflective of "the eternal urge of desire" that works "strongly and quietly by love," to guide the course of things within the world into "the creative advance into novelty." For Hartshorne, by contrast, God is less an active force within the world's processual commerce than an intelligent being or mind that interacts with it. His God is less a force of some sort than a personal being who interacts with the other mind-endowed agents through personal contact and love. Hartshorne wants neither to separate God from the world too sharply nor yet to have him be pantheistically immanent in nature. He views God as an intelligent world-separated being who participates experientially in everything that occurs in nature and resonates with it in experiential participation.

Such differences of approach, however, are only of secondary importance. The crucial fact is that the stratagem of conceiving of God in terms of a *process* that is at work in and beyond the world makes it possible to overcome a whole host of substance-geared difficulties with one blow. For it now becomes far easier to understand how God can be and be operative. To be sure, the processual view of God involves a recourse to processes of a very special kind. But extraordinary (or even supranatural) *processes* pose far fewer difficulties than extraordinary (or let alone supranatural) *substances*, seeing that process is an inherently more flexible conception. After all, many sorts of processes are in their own way unique—or, at any rate, radically different from all others. Clearly, processes like the creation of a world or the inauguration of its lawful order are by their very nature bound to be unusual, but much the same can be said of any particular type of process. Moreover, through its recourse to the idea of a megaprocess that embraces and encompasses a variety of subordinate processes, process theology is able to provide a conceptual rationale for reconciling the idea of an all-pervasive and omnitemporal mode of reality with that of a manifold of finitely temporalized constituents.[4]

The processist view of nature as a spatiotemporal whole constituting one vast, all-embracing cosmic process unfolding under the directive aegis of a benign intelligence is, in various ways, in harmony with the Judeo-Christian view of things. For this tradition has always seen God as active within the historical process which, in consequence, represents not only a causal but also a purposive order. After all, the only sort of God who can have meaning and significance for us is one who stands in some active interrelationship with ourselves and our world. (Think here of the Nicene creed's phraseology: "the maker of all things . . . who for us men and for our salvation. . . .") But, of course, such an "active interrelationship" is a matter of the processes that constitute the participation and entry of the divine into the world's scheme of things—and conversely.

And, of course, not only is it feasible and potentially constructive for the relation of God to the world and its creatures to be conceived of in terms of processes, but it is so also with the relationship of people to God. Here, too, process theology sees such a relationship as thoroughly processual because it rests on a potentially interactive communion established in contemplation, worship, prayer, and the like.

In particular, for processists, there is little difficulty in conceiving God as a *person*. For once we have an account of personhood in general in process terms as a systemic complex of characteristic activities, it is no longer all that strange to see

God in these terms as well. If we processify the human person, then we can more readily conceive of the divine person as the focal source of a creative intelligence that engenders and sustains the world and endows it with law, beauty (harmony and order), value, and meaning.

Then, too, there is the problem of the Trinity with its mystery of fitting three persons into one being or substance, which has always been a stumbling block for the substantialism of the Church Fathers. A process approach makes it possible to bypass this perplexity, for processes can conflate with and interpenetrate one another. With the laying of a single branch, a woodsman can be building a wall, erecting a house, and extending a village: one act, many processes; one mode of activity, many sorts of agency.

For process theology, then, God is active in relation to the world, and the world's people can and should be active in relation to God. People's relationship to the divine is a two-way street, providing for a benevolent God's care for the world's creatures and allowing those intelligent beings capable of realizing this to establish contact with God through prayer, worship, and spiritual communion. Process theology accordingly contemplates a wider realm of processes that embrace both the natural and the spiritual realms and interconnect God with the vast community of worshippers in one communal macroprocess that encompasses and gives embodiment to such a communion.

3. God in Time and Eternity: The Problem of Free Will

The relation of God to time and its changes provides another focal theme for process theology. Proceeding under the aegis of the substance paradigm of Greek philosophy, the Church Fathers placed God outside time in a distinctive order of eternity. And here the question arises about how God can know—let alone comfort and commiserate with—the condition of beings existing in time. Saint Thomas here used the explanatory analogy of the spectator on a mountain watching the movement of travelers along the road in a valley below: The travelers cannot see around the twists and turns in the road to know what lies before them, but God, looking down from eternity, can see the whole in a single glance, all at once (*totum simul*). But, of course, any prospect of contingency or of innovation is blocked out on this picture, save as the misimpression of imperfect humans; as with the theologies of Calvin or Spinoza, all that ever happens is foreseeable and, indeed, foreseen—everything is provided for from the start, so to speak. The process theologian rejects any such radical separation of God and world in the interests of making what William James called ontological "elbow room" for contingency, innovation, and unpredictability. The processualists' deity is not the God of the great *omnis* (omnipotence, omniscience, omnibenevolence). To reemphasize: process theology envisions a God who, though not *of* the world, is nevertheless present *in* it in a way that renders him, too, subject to the temporality that pervades its domain.[5]

As theologians of this tendency see it, God's processual involvement in the world is of many sorts, preeminently productive, cognitive, and affective. Divine providence furnishes the reason for being of the world's intelligible order, and is God himself linked to created nature by cognitive processes of awareness and understanding. Moreover, God is linked to the world of created beings through a reciprocity of affective appreciation, and responds to the world's eventuation by way of approbation or disapproval. (But what sorts of things in "his" world can God possibly approve or disapprove of? This sphere would have to include the doings of autonymous agencies that "go their own way", including, most importantly, some of the free actions of intelligent creatures.)

Yet if—as most processists agree—divine intelligence can know about human free actions, then what becomes of our freedom of choice and will? Processists construe God's omniscience in terms of his knowing everything that *can* be known, and regard human free actions as involving—at least sometimes—matters that cannot be known in advance of the fact. About such matters God, like the rest of us, can only learn in the fullness of time. (For processists, time is so potent a factor that even God is not wholly its master.) Process theologians accordingly incline to look with favor on Faustus Socinus

(Fausto Paolo Sozzini, 1539–1604) who maintained that human freedom is incompatible with divine foreknowledge of our free acts and that—since free action is an accomplished fact—there has to be room for a *change* in God (in particular, in respect to his knowledge) that is consequent upon the course of events. To be sure, God is omniscient and gets to know everything—but only in due course. On this basis, processists abandon the idea of God's immutability along with that of a total separation from the world's developments. From the angle of traditional Christian doctrines, the piety of process religiosity may be altogether orthodox, but its theology is not, the processists link between God and nature being somewhat too intimate.

4. GOD IN AND FOR NATURE

With Laplace, the processist can say regarding God as explainer of the observed world, "We have no need for that hypothesis" (*Nous n'avons pas besoin de cette hypothèse*). For him, the service that God renders us is not so much to make the world *explicable* as to provide an incentive for finding it *appreciable* and for endeavoring to make it more so.

Nature may well, in the end, prove to be explanatorily self-contained. Individually and seriatim, the world's particular phenomena can presumably all be accounted for in terms of nature's own processes, and no super- or supranatural agency need be invoked. But explaining the phenomena of nature and appreciating them in terms of an apprehension of their worth and value are very different things. To be sure, the fact that people make evaluations is itself a natural phenomenon that has natural explanations. But the normative fact that (often) they do so rightly—that the things people factually prize are (often) normatively worth prizing—is something of a different order.

While process philosophers grant God a productive role in the world's realm of things, they see this less in terms of the efficient causality at issue with the scientific explanation of things than in terms of the final causality that endows the world with an axiological dimension by making a place for values in its idea of things. As process theology sees it, God is rather the source of *inspiration* for the world's agents than a basis of *explanation* for that they do.

The presence of arrangements in the world *that we like and that please us* can be explained naturally with reference to biological evolutions: attunement of creatures to their environment. But the fact that the world's arrangements *have worth and value in and of themselves* cries out for reference to the divine. And here process theology takes its hold. The service it sees the divine as rendering to human understanding does not lie in the order of causal explanation but rather in the order of evaluative appreciation—in enabling us to apprehend more correctly and realistically the grounds and indications of the fact that the world's arrangements can have worth and value.

The presence of chance, chaos, and choice on the world scene means that the course of the world's development poses genuine alternatives—contingently open possibilities where the course of events can run in one channel rather than another. Things can evolve and eventuate for the better or for the worse. The course of physical, biological, and cultural evolution is strewn with endless contingencies. The restrictive necessities of physical process no more mean that things need go well than the restrictive necessities of chess rules mean that the game must be played well. The what and how of the world's course of happenings are some sort of (factual) thing, but their evaluative assessment is quite another (normative) one. The presence of value in a world of chance may not *demand* belief in a benign directive influence at work within the world's processual flux (it could all be "pure luck"), but it certainly *invites* it.

We live in a world where there is not only *change* but also *progress* (= change for the better)—which, as we have seen, is geared to the process of evolution in its various manifestations. And this higher-level normative fact may be explained in terms of a three-cornered relationship between God, the world, and the intelligently evaluative beings that exist within it. The workings of evolution—cosmic, biological, and social— are all natural processes that operate in and through the world's sphere of contingency and chance. But the (evaluative) fact that these processes function so as to yield something that has value is a circumstance which, as process theology sees it, profoundly manifests the presence of a benign intelligence at work in or through the phenomena of nature. As process theology sees it, it is in this relationship to the world as a locus of value, rather than to it as a manifold of phenomena, that the hand of God upon the world's processes manifests itself most strikingly.

To be sure, process philosophers differ from one another regarding the notion of God. Some take an immanentist line and view the divine as a force or factor at work within the cosmic processes to make for an ongoing enhancement of intelligible order and appreciable value. Others take a more transcendentist line and view the divinity as a processual being or entity—a superprocess of sorts that works upon, rather than within, the world's constitutive machine of processes. (Thus Whitehead admitted that while he called God a "principle of concretion," he did not really mean to call God a principle but rather an actual entity that gives operative endowment to such a principle.[6])

Yet while processists differ regarding the nature of God, they generally agree that the proper appreciation of the natural sphere and its modus operandi involves recourse to a world-transcendent factor—that from an axiological point of view nature cannot be seen as a wholly self-contained and autonomous realm. A proper appreciation of the real accordingly involves reference to something extra- if not supranatural. So far, so good. But from a traditional Judeo-Christian standpoint, processists incline to the unorthodoxy of seeing God as a power rather than as a person—and, indeed, a power that, just like the world, incorporates real potentiality in its make-up.

It is not that process theology proposes to worship a different God or puts forward a different creed. In point of forms and formalities it is (or can be) perfectly orthodox. What is at issue is a matter of the interpretation or construction of the traditional formulas that the process approach makes available. No radical lapse from tradition need be envisioned here. Process theology can take a position that is not so much revisionist as explanatory; its line can be that of the question, If a God along the traditional lines exists, then how can a being of this sort be most effectively (most intelligibly and least problematically) conceptualized?"

In the final reckoning, then, the process approach has some distinct advantages for theology over against a substance approach. Specifically, it makes it easier and less problematic to understand the nature of God as a person and this being's participating role in relation to the world. The process approach thus affords a framework for conceiving of God in a way that not only removes many of the difficulties inherent in the thing-oriented, substantial approach of traditional metaphysics but also makes it vastly easier to provide a philosophical rationale for many—though not all—of the leading conceptions of Judeo-Christian religiosity.

10

Process in Philosophy

SYNOPSIS

(1) The philosophy of process is also a philosophy in process. It is not a definitively stabilized position, but a changing and evolving program whose nature must itself be understood in processual terms. (2) Process philosophy is thus self-consistent; it represents itself as a philosophy-in-process that does not seek to impose a procrustean conceptual stability. (3) And this is all to the good. For metaphilosophy—the philosophical study of philosophy itself—is well advised to see philosophy in processual terms. (4) All in all, then, the process approach both in and to philosophy enjoys a variety of assets and advantages over traditional substantialism that indicate that it merits close and sympathetic attention.

1. PHILOSOPHY IN PROCESS

Confidence in the interest and utility of the metaphysical enterprise in its more or less traditional configuration is a salient aspect of the optimistic outlook of process philosophy. Most of the major philosophical movements of the twentieth century have (from a variety of very different perspectives) insisted upon the inappropriateness of metaphysics. Think here of the scientism of logical positivism, the rigid empiricism of linguistic analysis, the negativity of Heideggerian hermeneutics, the nihilism of neo-Nietzschean postmodernism, the anticognitivism of neopragmatism, the know-nothing prosaicism of the later Wittgenstein. One after another, the avant garde movements of twentieth-century philosophy have abandoned the problems of traditional metaphysics as reflecting the outmoded concerns and conceptions of a bygone era. However, process philosophy firmly sets itself against all of this negativism. It yields to no one in point of appreciating the fruits of scientific and cultural studies. But it sees in them not a substitute for traditional philosophizing but rather a source of grist for philosophy's mill. Against the current of the age, process philosophy does not see science or logic or language theory or artificial intelligence as providing *replacements* for philosophy as traditionally conceived, but regards all of these enterprises as enriching the agenda of issues and as furnishing materials for productive philosophy.

To be sure, it would be a mistake to regard process metaphysics as a complete and definitively constituted doctrinal position rather than as an "approach" (as we have generally characterized it here). For that philosophy *of* process is also a philosophy *in* process. It is not a doctrinal framework of fixed conceptual stability but a changing and evolving approach whose nature must itself be understood in processual terms. Yet is this line of thought actually coherent? Can a consistent theory of philosophy at once elaborate its claims and concede their limitations?

2. IS PROCESS PHILOSOPHY COHERENT?

Process philosophers are sometimes accused of inconsistency. They are presented with this challenge: How can you say that everything changes and that the world has no permanent features when this condition of ever-changingness and impermanence is itself (according to your own theory) a permanent feature of reality?

The fact is that process philosophy's emphasis on the ubiquity of change has to be understood with some degree of sophistication. We cannot simply say that "everything changes" and just let it go at that. Change is, first and foremost, the moving frontier that separates the past and the future and thereby characterizes the productive present. The past as such does not change; it changes only through its relationships to what comes after. The letter *S* remains one selfsame letter, but it is differentiated in operative effect when followed by *IT* and by *AD*. This sort of change may be a "second-order" change (a "Cambridge change," as some philosophers have called it), but it is a change all the same. A certain sophistication is called for here. And, in particular, one must recognize that a change *in* process philosophy is not necessarily a change *of* process philosophy.

Yet given the comparative stability of linguistic assertion, how can we capture a realm of process within the fixities of language and logic? This is an old complaint. With a view to Zeno's paradoxes, Aristotle already argued that a doctrine that contends that everything changes—always and anywhere both is and is not—stands in violation of the principle of non-contradiction and is consequently incoherent. And, indeed, the claim that everything changes does itself have a look of expediently self-excepting fixity about it.

But appearances are misleading here. The matter is not quite so grave. For one must heed the distinction between the domain of facts with which a theory deals and the domain of facts to which the theory belongs. Botany deals with plants, but a botanical principle is not itself a plant. Meteorology deals with the weather, but is not itself a meteorological phenomenon. Similarly, a metaphysical position as such is not itself part of the phenomena of nature, and accordingly need not fall within the scope of its own immediate concerns. In saying that *everything within* nature changes, we need not deny that certain *facts about* nature (such as "Everything in nature changes") may themselves hold changelessly true. To be sure, people's views and contentions regarding the issues of process philosophy are natural phenomena. And if process philosophy is right, then these beliefs will change and develop over time, as will the interpretation and understanding of those all too stable looking theses by which we formulate them. But, of course, it is a well-confirmed fact of life, rather than a paradox, that the historical course of things brings about changes in people's views about any theory—be it the atomic theory of matter or the theory of natural progress at large.

To some extent, however, the complaint has merit. The philosophy of process is also a philosophy in process. As yet, we do not have a fully developed and adequately articulated process philosophy in hand. For all that has been said and done by its exponents in various places and times, process philosophy is still in many ways incomplete and imperfect. But, of course, much the same complaint could be made against any and every approach in metaphysics. And in this regard, process philosophy at least has the virtue of self-substantiation. As one acute commentator has noted, "The unfinished and never-to-be-finished quality of (processual) flux has seduced many adherents to the metaphysics of process among systematic theory building."[1] True to the spirit of its own approach, process philosophy can and does see itself not as a finished product but as an ongoing project of inquiry.

Insofar as process philosophy is true to itself, it will have to proceed in its own terms of reference. For a processist to hold that it has arrived at a fully fixed set of categories or a definitive array of explanating principles would be treason to the spirit of the enterprise. The complexity and volatility of experience precludes finality. A framework of thought that is to be adequate to experience must forgo claims to completeness, for the very idea of definitive correctness—of achieving at once the generality and precision that is desired—is rendered infeasible by philosophy's unavoidable reliance on imperfect instrument of human language. All philosophizing is a matter of imperfect approximation.

Accordingly, no particular discussion of process philosophy should be seen as presenting a finished and definitively articulated presentation of the doctrine. Any such discussion, the present one emphatically included, should regard and present itself in the process-congenial manner "not . . . of finality but of progress," as Whitehead put it.[2] It would, in fact, perhaps be preferable to speak of process philosophizing rather than process philosophy, using here, too, the language of activity rather than of things.

3. THE STATE OF PROCESS PHILOSOPHY

As we have seen, the process approach has played a significant part in Anglo-American thought—in particular, in relation to pragmatic philosophy and to naturalistic theology. But what about critique? By rights, one would expect there to be a substantial body of critical eventuations or even refutations of process philosophizing. But this expectation will be disappointed. Interestingly enough, the student looking for elaborate evaluations and detailed criticisms of process thought will come away disappointed. While process ontology itself is a critical position that finds its reason for being in the critique and refutation of a substantialist approach, it itself has not undergone much critical examination. Those who are disinclined to its teachings have simply gone their own way, elaborating as best they can their own substance-oriented positions without worrying about the processual alternative processists.

The main exception to this rule is one that was examined at length above—namely, P. F. Strawson's putative refutation of processism in his influential book, *Individuals*,[3] which does indeed subject fundamental commitments of process philosophy to a frontal-assault critique. But one swallow does not make a summer, and this one exception to the policy of criticism by neglect does not alter the overall situation as regards the fate of process philosophy on the contemporary scene. The fact remains that those who reject process philosophy have, for the most part, simply ignored it and have devoted themselves to the elaboration of alternative positions. Yet why should this be so?

Part of the reason for the phenomenon lies in the nature of process philosophy itself. As we have seen, it is rather a general line of approach than a particular philosophical thesis or theory. And this flexible and diffuse nature of the approach means that it presents an inauspicious target for criticism. Theses and theories are definite—they can be pinned down and critically dissected. But approaches are too plastic, too mercurial to admit conveniently of critical evaluation.

Then, too, another part of the reason lies in the processual nature of philosophy. Philosophy as a whole, viewed as a communal enterprise (rather than an individual position), consists in the ongoing exploration and development of different lines of approach. Accordingly, a philosopher's criticism of a theory is often indirect, proceeding through the elaboration of an alternative rival position that is seen as having more salient points of advantage and appeal. One relies on one's own philosophical hobby horse and hopes that those pesky rivals will simply go away. But of course they do not. Instead, they force their rival position to become enlarged, enhanced, and more sophisticated. Matters never come to a standstill. In philosophical debate there is no closure.

Be this as it may, however, the fact remains that process philosophy has not, as yet, received the attention—and the opposition—that it deserves.

4. Process and Metaphilosophy

The deliberations of the book have sought to substantiate and illustrate the utility and feasibility of the process approach in philosophy. But it deserves to be noted and emphasized that it is a crucial feature of the philosophical enterprise that metaphilosophy—the theoretical study of philosophy and philosophizing—is part and parcel of philosophy itself. And so, insofar as processism is useful and appropriate in philosophy in general, a process-geared approach would also seem to be in order with respect to metaphilosophy. This expectation is, in fact, fully borne out by circumstances that prevail, seeing that philosophy is an ongoing process of conjecture that exploits the data of experience to resolve the "big questions" that represent the traditional focus of the enterprise. For experience is an ever-changing landscape—particularly in the present context of philosophical experience, where the deliverances of past philosophizing always form part of that experience to which present philosophizing must address itself. A process-oriented view of philosophizing is accordingly very much in order.

Upon death, a philosopher's life and work is something fixed and finished, something inert, dead, and catalogable—the stuff of historical expositions and reference works and library collections. However, we must distinguish between a text and the ideas at work within it, between the particular formulations of particular philosophers and the operative philosophical ideas, problems, doctrines, controversies, and the like that are at issue in their work. In philosophy, we do well to separate process and product, discriminating between philosophizing as an ongoing enterprise on the one side and a fixed philosophical artifact (book or article or lecture) on the other. For as an ongoing enterprise the fact is that philosophy is best understood in process terms—in terms of the pondering dialectic of reflection, discussion, and exposition in the living process that produces those (comparatively) stable artifacts.

To be sure, we have to make use those texts (i.e., linguistic productions) to get at the ideational processes at issue. But all the same, the nature of philosophy is best viewed in terms of process—of active philosophizing in relation to the continuing disputes and discussions that represent the actual activities of the community of working philosophers. Philosophy is a venture in inquiry within which the ideas at work in these historical artifacts (those inert-seeming texts) are transmuted into the stuff of living thought through which the ideas at issue are developed, refined, interrelated, and so forth. It is, then, as an ongoing venture in cognitive adaptation to living experience and as an inherently dynamic activity of inquiry that philosophy should be understood—as a matter of ongoingly readjusting our answers to the "perennial questions" in the light of an ever-changing body of information and reflection. In sum, philosophy as such is less an object than a process; its crux is not the stable formulation of intentions but the active, living development and interplay of ideas.

Moreover, philosophizing is a teleological process; it is designed with an end in view. For, as has been stressed throughout these deliberations, philosophy is a purposive enterprise aimed at problem solving, at providing answers to our questions regarding the world's scheme of things and our place within it. Since human life, individual or collective, is itself an ever-changing process or situation in the world's scheme, this must also be the case with the articulation of a philosophical perspective that reflects upon it in the endeavor to bring theory and experience into alignment.

Accordingly, any general philosophical position or doctrine is in itself something unfinished, incomplete, and obsolescent.

Every philosopher's teachings are bound to be superseded by other, enhanced and improved versions that, through exploiting larger views and ampler experiences, make it possible to realize a more sophisticated insight into the particular persistent line of thought or intellectual tradition that is at issue. Throughout philosophy, the presently attained stage is not the end of the road—the journey continues ever onwards—though it could not proceed on its actual course had its present stage not been attained. And this developmental and processive aspect of process philosophy itself is essential to its viability as a productive intellectual enterprise. For any philosophy that does not allow the development, extension, and growth essential to an ongoing tradition is destined to become a mere fossil, a museum piece rather than a living force.

5. THE BOTTOM LINE

The conflict between the approaches of substance and process metaphysics is clearly not an issue that can be resolved one way or the other by decisive theoretical argumentation. In the end, the issue will be one of cost–benefit analysis, of comparing the net balance of the assets and liabilities of the two approaches. And here processism compares favorably with substance philosophy—not just in providing a natural and plausible account of the "nature of things" but by coming to terms in a more realistic way with issues of identity, individuation, and unification, as well as of coming to be and passing away. The concept-mechanisms that are natural and intrinsic to process philosophy enable us to resolve the problems that must be addressed by any adequate metaphysics, and they do so in a manner that is arguably less strained and less cumbersome than that of its substantialist rival. Process theory's insistence on the processual nature of concrete particulars may well be unorthodox from the angle of the substantialist mainstream of Western philosophical tradition. But that does not prevent there being much to recommend it.

But what of the bottom line? Why should the process philosophy approach be entertained in a serious and sympathetic way?

As with most philosophical disputes, the prospect of set-
tling the issue by decisive, knock-down, drag-out argumentation is somewhere between minuscule and nonexistent. The
best one can do is to effect an overall comparison to show that
there is a favorable net balance of theoretical advantages.
These have been set out step-by-step in the preceding discussion, and it is appropriate to review them here:

- Substance, insofar as we can develop a cogent theoretic
  account of the matter, cannot be freed from a recourse to
  process (neither as regards its inner nature nor as
  regards our knowledge of it).
- A rigorously construed substance metaphysics cannot as
  such explain agency and change, whereas processes are
  by nature self-potentiating and issue further processes
  (i.e., changes).
- Moreover, a process approach to the nature and existence of substances can be successfully implemented.
- The identity and identification of substance is inextrica-
  bly bound up with the occurrence of processes.
- The process approach averts or minimizes the difficulties
  inherent in the traditional problem of universals.
- The process perspective is smoothly attuned to and substantially consonant with the view of nature (physical, biological, and social) that is articulated in modern science.
- The process approach provides a more natural account
  of persons and personhood than the substance approach
  makes available.
- The process approach yields an explanation of acquisition, development, and management of information in a
  way that gives process epistemology marked advantages.
- The process approach provides an effective framework for
  better understanding both the conduct and product of
  rational inquiry.
- Process theology makes it possible to avert some of the
  perplexities and theoretical anomalies of a substance
  approach to God.
- The nature of philosophy and philosophizing itself is best
  understood as the basis of a process perspective.

As these deliberations have sought to indicate, the process approach provides a resource of substantial utility throughout the philosophical domain. Even if it did no more than provide a contrast case that highlights various conceptual and philosophical difficulties that confront a substance approach to metaphysics, it would still render a substantial service. But process philosophy does substantially more than this, since it not only illuminates those problems and difficulties of substance philosophy but also provides an instrument for addressing them in the search for tenable resolutions.

The paramount value of process metaphysics, however, lies in its providing not just a means to avert various philosophical difficulties but a distinctive and illuminating window on the world. For this approach has an importantly true-to-reality aspect. It invites us to regard what we see when we look about us, not in the light of an aggregation of perduring things but in that of a vibrant manifold of productive activity. It pictures the world not as a museum where objects are displayed but as a show where things happen—a theater, as it were, in full productive stir. In this way, it offers an instructive and productive alternative to the substantialist approach that has left its deeply problematic imprint upon mainstream philosophical tradition.

The perfection of a possible world consists, according to Leibniz, in the extent to which it can combine variety and order, detail and comprehensiveness. Be this as it may with respect to worlds, it remains true with respect to philosophical systems, whose adequacy consists in exactly the extent to which they facilitate an understanding of details within a framework of comprehensive inclusiveness. And just here lies the merit that process philosophers claim for their approach.[4] Whether this is indeed so in this particular case is something that readers will have to judge for themselves. It clearly will not do to let processists be judges in their own cause. But it is, at any rate, by this standard that the metaphysics of process, like any other, must be assessed.

Appendix: Process Semantics

The development of a process semantics is important for substantiating the claims of process philosophy because it enables the process philosopher to counter the following challenge:

> Logic is surely the conceptually most versatile (and philosophically most fundamental) of intellectual enterprises. But the most fully developed logic we have—classical quantificational logic—is based on the substance semantics of Russell and Tarski and Quine. You process theorists have no alternative to this. You are in the anomalous and uncomfortable position of having to conduct your reasoning with an instrumentality developed on the basis of your opponent's doctrines.

To meet this objection it must be shown that—and how—a process semantics can be developed. The present discussion gives a few indications as to how this might be done. To try for more within the confines of a brief appendix would be impractical.

Communicative meanings have their existence through the symbolic processes at work in our processual linguistic practices of assertion and denial, of substantiation and invalidation, of evidence and refutation, of conjecture and inference. Meanings accordingly arise in and operate through the procedures that we use in conveying and in processing information. But, of course, we can communicate meaningfully not just about what is but also about what is not but is merely conceivable, so that the realm of meaning is far wider than that of reality. Now, in this context, the idea of nonexistent individuals has long troubled subject–predicate theorists.[1]

The focal problem here is posed by the question, How can there possibly be a namable, identifiable, discussible individual—such as the winged horse Pegasus—that does not actually exist? To talk about something is surely somehow to claim its reality; after all, in standard logic a contention F regarding an item a, symbolically "$F(a)$," is equivalent to "$(\exists x)(x = a \& F(x))$." As Parmenides already insisted, to be discussible is already a matter of somehow being—to be as an object is already in some way or other to be. But if this is so, how can we then avoid the awkward consequence that the truistic-looking premiss

winged horse (Pegasus) $\cong$ Pegasus is a winged horse

does not yield the patently false conclusion

$(\exists x)x$ is a winged horse $\cong$ There is a winged horse?

The well-known Theory of Descriptions which Bertrand Russell projected at the dawn of the twentieth century endeavored to resolve this problem within the framework of subject–predicate logic, but it ran into various technical difficulties which need not be detailed here. (Russell's analysis made it impossible to speak truth about nonexistents; on its basis it is equally false to say "The present king in France is canine" and "The present king of France is fictitious.")

To avert these and other problems, W. V. O. Quine proposed in the 1950s the interesting expedient of dispensing altogether with named individuals in semantical theory, replacing them with suitable "adjectives."[2] Dismissing the substantive *Pegasus*, we are to resort to the object description *pegasizer*. Named individuals as semantical items and nonexistent individuals disappear with them. Thus, on Quine's approach, we are to rephrase the equation "$x = a$" as a predication, where "$= a$" is taken as a general term—an adjective—so that "Pegasus is a winged horse" becomes the harmless truism, "Whatever answers to the object description of being a pegasizer (i.e., nothing) is a winged horse." In such cases, the singular term or name "comes to play the role of the 'F' in 'Fa' and ceases to play that of the 'a'"[3] In this vein, Quine speaks of an artificial and trivial-seeming device (which creates) the *ex hypothesi* unanalysable, irreducible attribute of *being Pegasus,.* . . . The noun 'Pegasus' itself could then be treated as derivative, and identified after all with a description: 'the thing that is-Pegasus', 'the thing that pegasizes'.[4]

The singular term for a nonexistent such as Pegasus is thus switched to a predicative position, so as to become a general descriptive term. We trade in that difficulty-engendering noun for a less problematic adjective. Pegasus simply vanishes as a "nonexistent *individual*," and a characteristic uninstantiated *descriptor* arises to take its place.

But Quine's proposed reconstruction leaves matters in a somewhat anomalous position. For his elimination of substantives in favor of adjectives does not, as he himself recognized, involve the actual elimination of objects to which such ex hypothesi noninstantiated predicates are (nominally) attributed: "the objects stay on as values of the variables though the singular terms be swept away."[5]

However, the interesting and noteworthy fact now comes to view that this uncomfortable halfway house can be abandoned if we shift to a process semantics. On such an approach, one would take the further step of trading *adjectives* in for *adverbs*. Specifically, one would look at "pegasizing" not as a characteristic attribute that represents a *property of individuals* but as a *process* that can transpire at various spatiotemporally positional coordinates[6]—that is, in different settings and contexts. What is characteristic of Pegasus is not that it is a pegasi*zer* but rather that it pegasi*zes*. And this pegasizing is now a very particular sort of process, and the object-neutral conception of "it pegasizes" is analogous to "it rains" or "it is hot" in that we must address the issue of where-and-when. The (false) statement "Pegasus exists" will be glossed as

$$(\exists p) \text{ (pegasizing at } p),$$

and the (true) statement "Pegasus does not exist" would be glossed as its denial

$$(\forall p) \sim (\text{pegasizing at } p),$$

where *p* is a *positional* variable (indicative of placement within a wider processual setting)—a contextual locator within an overreaching space–time framework. To deny the actual existence of something is not to deny its discussibility but rather to stipulate its exclusion from the realm context of the reals.

This semantical strategy, which dispenses with singular object/substance terms altogether and uses qualification as a merely positional device, can be carried over uniformly to actual existents as well. By parity of reasoning, one eliminates not only nonexistents such as Pegasus as (mysterious) objects but Quine's object descriptions as well. For, on this approach, one ceases to regard pegasizing as a thing-descriptive *adjective* and moves on to seeing it as a genuinely process-indicative *verb*. After all, what concretizes a particular instance of a physical process of a certain generic sort as a particular element of concrete reality is precisely its having such a place in the world's scheme of things. It is particularized through the operation of a certain sort of process of location placement (be it ostensive or descriptive in terms of a locational system such as coordinates). Every actual physical process conjoins a "positional" placement aspect with a "structural" type-classification aspect: It is both a *this* and a *what*. (Note that "adding 2 and 2" is not as such a concrete physical process but that Smith's adding 2 and 2 here and now is.)

In general, a process semantics should be—and is—in a position to accomplish with verbs and adverbs whatever a semantics of individuals can manage to do with properties and relations. When the one says "*X* has the property *F*", the other says "*X* functions *F*-ly" for some suitably *F*-corresponding process. (Thus, "*X* is triangular" becomes "*X* disports itself triangularly." And where the one says "*X* is north-of-*Y*" becomes "*X* locates itself to-the-north-of-*Y*-ly.)

Conveniently, this processual approach yields a uniform approach to existents and nonexistents, putting quining ("to quine") alongside of pegasizing ("to pegasize"). There is now no longer any need for a shadowy variable-range of nonnamable individuals, because one can straightforwardly operate with instances of verb-application. "It quines here" does duty for "Quine is here," and "It quines somewhere" replaces "Quine exists." "Quine is a philosopher"—that is, "Quine sometimes philosophizes"[7]—does not now represent the subject–predicate claim

philosopher (Quine)

Rather, it is now construed as the process-relating claim that Quine sometimes philosophizes, namely,

some philosophizings are (parts or aspects of) quinings

or more fully

$(\exists p)$ (it philosophizes at p & it quines at p & (it philosophizes at p @ it quines at p).

(Here @ represents *containment* or *inclusion* among processes and p is, as before, a variable that ranges over spatiotemporal positions.) Accordingly, the process semanticist treats *nonexistent* particulars and *actual* particulars alike—both are reflected in processes that may or may not be realized at coordinate reference positions.

This variant semantics makes it possible to overcome some familiar difficulties that affect the standard thing-property semantics. Consider, for example, Donald Davidson's well-known complaint that standard subject–predicate logic has difficulty in coming to terms with:

(1) X buttered the toast carefully and deliberately.

As he sees it, the closest one can come to formulate this by standard means is

(2) X buttered the toast carefully and X buttered the toast deliberately.

And Davidson now objects: "The trouble is that we have nothing here we would ordinarily recognize as a singular term. Another sign that we have not caught the logical form of the sentence is that in this last version there is no implication that any *one* act was both carefully and deliberate."[8]

But recourse to a semantics of processes serves to avert these difficulties. Thus, in rendering 1 we would first move to

(3) $(\exists y)$ (y is an action of buttering toast & y is an X-performed action & y is a careful action & y is a deliberate action).

And the final step in the rendition is to gloss that individual-object reference to X processually by making use of the equivalence

y is an X-performed action = $(\exists p)$ (it y's at p & it X's at p & (it y's at p @ it X's at p)).

We would accordingly arrive at

(4) $(\exists y)$ ((toast buttering (y) & $(\exists p)$ ((it y's at p & it X's at p) & (it y's at p @ it X's at p)) & careful action (y) & deliberate action (y))).

Observe (i) that there is now indeed something in this statement that "we would ordinarily recognize as a singular term," namely, "a (certain particular) toast buttering," and (ii) that the formation of 4 makes it clear that a single action is at issue throughout. Thus, in the language of processes, the formalization of 1 presents no particular obstacles. Its truth-conditions can be formulated more effectively in terms of processes and their relations than in terms of things and their properties.

An important collateral advantage of process semantics is that it affords a "natural" treatment of nonexistent individuals that manages to overcome in a direct and felicitous way the problems faced by the standard substance-based approaches. Of these there are primarily two.

Russell's Approach. Let x be a nonexistent individual (*say, the present king of France*), or, more generally, the-x

(*Fx*)—that is, the *x* such that *Fx*, where *F* is noninstantiated. Then, for Russell, the attribution of a property *G* to such an individual comes down to

$$G[\text{the-}x(Fx)] = (\exists x) \ [Fx \ \& \ (\forall y) \ (Fy \supset y = x) \ \& \ Gx].$$

That is, the-*x*(*Fx*) has *G* if exactly one thing has *F* and this thing has *G*. Accordingly, Russell's analysis renders *G*[the-*x*(*Fx*)] automatically and universally false, irrespective of the particular property *G* at issue. Thus, "The present king of France exists" is false, but so also is "The present king of France is inexistent" and "The present king of France is a king."

The Naive Approach. By contrast, consider what might be called the naive approach, based on

$$G[\text{the-}x(Fx)] = (\forall x)(\forall y) \ [(Fx \ \& \ Fy) \supset y = x \ \& \ (\forall z) \ (Fz \supset Gz)].$$

That is, the-*x*(*Fx*) has *G* if all the things that have *F* are identical and furthermore leave *G*. But this analysis renders *G*[the-*x*(*Fx*)] automatically and universally true, irrespective of the particular property *F* at issue. Thus, "The present king of France exists" and "The present king of France is female" are both true.

To meet the requirements of a plausible and commonsensical construal of *G*[the-*x*(*Fx*)], we clearly need an analysis that makes this thesis true or false depending on the relationship between the properties *F* and *G*. And just such an analysis is readily provided for by the approach of process semantics.

Let us begin by reviewing the machinery at our disposal here:

I. We have an overall set of positions Π consisting of the set Σ of spatiotemporal positions plus the null position ø. (*Note*: The variables p, p_1, p_2, . . . will range over positions.)

II. We have an array of processes. (*Note*: The variables f, g, h, . . . will range over processes.) These processes may be either absolute or dispositional. (*Note*: A dispositional process will be indicated with a slash. Thus f/g is the processual dispositon for f to be actualized given g.)

III. To indicate that the process f is realized at the position p, we shall write: f-at-p.

Putting this machinery to work, we make the following observations:

1. "Pegasus is existent" or "Pegasus exists" is to be rendered as "$(\exists p)$ $(p \neq \emptyset$ & pegasizing-at-$p)$." This is false.
2. "Pegasus is inexistent" or "Pegasus does not exist" is to be rendered as "$(\forall p)$ $(p \neq \emptyset \supset \sim$ (pegasizing-at-$p)$," or, equivalently, "$(\forall p)$ (pegasizes-at-p $\supset$ p $= \emptyset)$." This is true.
3. "Pegasus is a winged horse" is to be rendered as "$(\forall p)$ ([(winging + horsing)/pegasizing]-at-$p)$." This is true.
4. "Pegasus is a winged cow" is to be rendered as "$(\forall p)$ ([(winging + cowing)/pegasizing]-at-$p)$." This is false.

Thus, our recourse to dispositional processes accomplishes exactly the needed job of rendering predicational claims of the form $G[\text{the-}x(Fx)]$ contingently true or false *even with nonexistents*, depending on the nature of the relationship that retains between F and G.

As this brief sketch indicates, a semantics of processes is a feasible and useful resource that affords a ready means for overcoming some of the characteristic limitations, problems, and difficulties of a semantics of objects-and-attributes.

Notes

INTRODUCTION (PP. 1–5)

1. Quoted from Ralph Barton Perry, *The Thought and Character of William James, Briefer Version* (Cambridge, MA: Harvard University Press, 1948), 30.

2. In the interests of being faithful to the process tradition at large, it does not even represent, always and everywhere, the personal position of the author.

3. This is why various philosophers—process thinkers like Peirce and Whitehead included—have felt it necessary to develop a technical (and, from their readers' angle, often off-putting) vocabulary, in contrast to others who, like the latter Wittgenstein, despair of the capacity of speculative systematizations to address philosophical issues successfully. While pessimism is as problematic here as elsewhere, nevertheless Ockham's razor continues to cut effectively: Artificialities like entities are never to be multiplied beyond necessity.

1. HISTORICAL BACKGROUND (PP. 7–26)

1. Many influential Whitehead scholars agree that the master's work must be seen in a broader context and that process philosophy is something larger than Whiteheadianism. In this category one may class William Christian Jr., George L. Kline, George R. Lucas, Jr., and Donald W. Sherburne, among others. (For their writings see the bibliography in this volume.)

2. G. S. Kirk, J. E. Raven, and M. Schofield, *The Presocratic Philosophers*, 2d ed. (Cambridge: Cambridge University Press, 1983), frag. 217. (Henceforth cited parenthetically by fragment number.) This book gives an informative account of the philosophy of Heraclitus. See also Dennis Sweet, *Heraclitus: Translation and Analysis* (Lanham, MD: University Press of America, 1995).

3. A good general account of Plato's philosophy is A. E. Taylor, *Plato: The Man and His Work* (London: Macmillan, 1926; 3d ed., rev. and enlarged, 1929).

4. Observe also that the epistemological views attributed to Protagoras in Plato's *Theaetetus* (see esp. 166B) are thoroughly processualistic.

5. A good general account of Aristotle's work is W. D. Ross, *Aristotle* (London: Methuen, 1923; 5th ed., rev., 1949).

6. For a general account of Leibniz's philosophy see Nicholas Rescher, *Leibniz: An Introduction to His Philosophy* (Oxford: Blackwell 1979; reissued, Ipswich: Gregg Revivals, 1993).

7. Two good general accounts of Hegel's philosophy are J. N. Findlay, *Hegel: A Reexamination* (Oxford: Oxford University Press, 1958); and Charles Taylor, *Hegel* (Cambridge: Cambridge University Press, 1975).

8. See Carl R. Hausman, *Charles S. Peirce's Evolutionary Philosophy* (Cambridge: Cambridge University Press, 1993).

9. "Not only may generals be real but they may be *physically efficient* . . . in the common-sense acceptation in which human purposes are physically efficient." (C. S. Peirce, *Collected Papers*, ed. Charles Hartshorne and Paul Weiss [Cambridge, MA: Harvard University Press, 1934], vol. 5, sect. 5.431).

10. For accounts of Peirce's philosophy see Thomas A. Goudge, *The Thought of Charles Sanders Peirce* (Toronto: University of Toronto Press, 1950); and Murray G. Murphey, *The Development of Peirce's Philosophy* (Cambridge, MA: Harvard University Press, 1961).

11. See William James, *The Principles of Psychology*, 2 vols. (New York: Henry Holt, 1890).

12. William James, *A Pluralistic Universe* (New York: Longmans Green, 1909), 122.

13. Ibid., 117.

14. Ibid., 153.

15. Ibid.

16. William James, "A World of Pure Experience," in *Essays in Radical Empiricism* (New York: Longmans Green, 1912), p. 54.

17. William James, *Principles of Psychology*, 1: 228.

18. A compact exposition of James' philosophy is given in Elizabeth Flower and Murray G. Murphey, *A History of Philosophy in America* (New York: G. P. Putnam's Sons, 1977), 635–792. A fuller account is Gerald E. Meyers, *William James: His Life and Thoughts* (New Haven: Yale University Press, 1986).

19. Henri Bergson, *Time and Free Will*, trans. F. L. Pogson (London: Macmillan, 1913), 101.

20. See Henri Bergson, *Creative Evolution* (New York: Henry Holt, 1911). However, evolutionist philosophers like C. Lloyd Morgan, while akin to process philosophers in some of their emphasis—especially the emergence of novelty—nevertheless represent a different tendency of thought. To be a process metaphysician is not just to see change and novelty at work in the large (in the cosmic or biological or social realms). It calls for taking the processual view not just of the macrocosm but of the microcosm as well.

21. For Bergson's philosophy see H. W. Carr, *Henri Bergson: The Philosophy of Change* (London: T. C. and E. C. Jack, 1911); and J. M. Stewart, *A Critical Exposition of Bergson's Philosophy* (London: Macmillan, 1911).

22. J. A. Boydston and B. A. Walsh (eds.), *The Middle Works of John Dewey* (Carbondale: Southern Illinois University Press, 1988), 223.

23. John Dewey, *Time and Its Mysteries* (New York: New York University Press, 1940), 155.

24. Ibid., 157.

25. Ibid.

26. For Dewey's philosophy see George R. Geiger, *John Dewey in Perspective* (Oxford: Oxford University Press, 1958). See also P. A. Schilpp (ed.), *The Philosophy of John Dewey* (La Salle, IL: Open Court, 1939).

27. The masthead policy statement for the journal *Process Philosophy* declares, "Process philosophy may be defined as applying principally, though not exclusively, to the philosophy of Alfred North Whitehead and his intellectual associates."

28. A. N. Whitehead, *The Concept of Nature* (Cambridge: Cambridge University Press, 1920), chap. 3.

29. A. N. Whitehead, *Science and the Modern World* (New York: Macmillan, 1925), 106.

30. A. N. Whitehead, *Process and Reality*, 80/124. *Process and Reality* was initially published in 1929 by Macmillan in London. A corrected edition, edited by David Ray Griffin and Donald W. Sherburne, was published in New York by The Free Press in 1978. References to this work are here given by the page numbers of both editions, with the latter edition first.

31. Ibid., 318/471.

32. A compressed but informative account of Whitehead's thought is given in Bruce Kuklick, *The Rise of American Philosophy* (New Haven: Yale University Press, 1977).

33. The former linkage is brought to light especially in the books of George R. Lucas Jr. (see the bibliography), and the latter linkage is illustrated in the present volume.

34. Bruce Kuklick, *Rise of American Philosophy*, 532. To be sure, Whitehead's reception among later philosophers in the Anglo-American analytic tradition was cool. See George R. Lucas Jr., "Whitehead and Wittgenstein," in J. Hintikka and K. Puhl (eds.), *Ludwig Wittgenstein and the Twentieth-Century British Tradition in Philosophy* (Vienna: Verlag Hölder-Pickler-Tempsky, 1995; Proceedings of the 17th International Wittgenstein Congress, Vienna, 1994). For a good appreciation of Whitehead's position in the history of modern thought and of the relevancy of his work for contemporary philosophy, see George R. Lucas Jr., *The Rehabilitation of Whitehead* (Albany, NY: SUNY Press, 1989).

35. See, in particular, Sheldon's *The Strife of Systems and Productive Duality: An Essay in Philosophy* (Cambridge: Harvard University Press, 1918); and W. H. Sheldon, *Process and Polarity* (New York: Columbia University Press, 1944).

36. Sheldon, *Process and Polarity*, 118.

37. Sheldon, *Strife of Systems and Productive Duality*, 478–79.

38. Here Sheldon harks back to the key thesis of Heraclitus, the initiator of process philosophy, who saw the real as "an attunement of opposing tensions, like that of the harp and the lyre" (Kirk-Raven-Schofield, frag. 209).

39. *Op cit.*, 13.

40. Other examples include Andrew Paul Ushenko's *Power and Events* (Princeton: Princeton University Press, 1946); and Wilfred Sellars' "Foundations of a Metaphysics of Pure Process," *Monist* 64 (1987): 3–90.

41. For details, see the bibliography in this volume.

42. Gérard Deledalle, *La Philosophie Américaine* (Lausanne: L'Age d'Homme, 1983); see 265–66.

2. BASIC IDEAS (PP. 27–49)

1. And time itself must be understood in terms of change rather than the other way around. Compare Aristotle, *Physics* IV.11 and Wittgenstein, *Tractatus* 6.3611.

2. See Mario Bunge, *Treatise on Basic Philosophy* (Dordrecht: Reidel, 1977), 1: 274–75.

3. For a fuller elabcration of this theme see Donald Hawks, "Process as a Categorical Concept," in R. C. Whittemore (ed.), *Studies in Process Philosophy II* (New Orleans: Tulane University Press, 1975).

4. Robert C. Whittemore, *Studies in Process Philosophy II*, 89–90. To these might be added: Whitehead, individuality.

5. This question is raised in Andrew J. Reck's interesting discussion, "Process Philosophy: A Categorical Analysis," in R. C. Whittemore (ed.), *Studies in Process Philosophy II*, 58–91.

6. James, *Principles of Psychology*, 1: 243.

7. This is particularly stressed in George Herbert Mead's Carus lectures on *The Philosophy of the Present* (Chicago: University of Chicago Press, 1972).

8. Whitehead, *Process and Reality*, 267–78/176–77. The experienced-feeling aspect of causal efficacy is particularly stressed in A. N. Ushenko, *Power and Events*. The "active geared principles" of causal power is also the crux of C. S. Peirce's "Harvard Experiment" (Collected Papers, 5.93–5.101).

3. PROCESS AND PARTICULARS (PP. 51–67)

1. See Locke's *Essay concerning Human Understanding*, bk. II, sect. xxiii.

2. G. W. F. Hegel, *Encyclopedia*, sect. 352, addendum.

3. Whitehead, *Process and Reality*, 20/30. "The real actual things that endure are all societies. They [viz. enduring things] are not actual occasions [which are always shortlived]" (A. N. Whitehead, *Adventures of Ideas* [New York: Macmillan, 1933], 262). For Whitehead, both physical things (trees, tables, cats) and subatomic particles are alike "corpuscular societies." For a more thoroughgoing processist, they could all be seen as simply constellations of process.

4. Peirce, *Collected Papers*, vol. 6, sect. 6.169.

5. Ibid., sect. 6.170.

6. On the issues at stake here, see the author's *Conceptual Idealism* (Oxford: Blackwell, 1973).

7. Whitehead, *Process and Reality*, 309/471.

8. P. F. Strawson, *Individuals: An Essay in Descriptive Metaphysics* (London: Methuen, 1959).

9. Ibid., 30.

10. Ibid.

11. The reasoning presented here is a somewhat abbreviated version of that presented in Johanna Seibt's "Towards Process Ontology" (Ph.D. diss., University of Pittsburgh, 1990), 303 ff.

12. On the relevant methodology, see the author's *The Strife of Systems* (Pittsburgh: University of Pittsburgh Press, 1985).

13. See the fuller discussion of these issues in the present author's essay "Exits from Paradox" in his *Satisfying Reason and Other Essays on the Philosophy of Knowledge* (Dordrecht: D. Reidel, 1995).

14. For a good popular account, see Dan McNeill, *Fuzzy Logic* (New York: Simon & Schuster, 1993).

15. There is a substantial literature on this subject and much of it surveyed in the author's *Introduction to Many-Valued Logic*

(New York: McGraw-Hill, 1969; Aldershot, UK, Gregg Revivals, 1993).

16. For further details see the author's essay, "Truth Value Gaps and Aristotelian Metaphysics," in *Satisfying Reason* (op. cit.).

4. PROCESS AND UNIVERSALS (PP. 69–82)

1. Nor—as the *Sophist* shows—was Plato himself unqualifiedly confident that process does not make its way into the realm of ideas itself.

2. A word about the nature of the structures at issue is in order. The events that constitute a process must be temporally coordinated in a programmatic structure. But they need not be *causally* connected. In the setting of the ancien régime, the king's formal morning toilette was a highly stylized process of etiquette. He arises, washes, is handed his clothes by the attendant wardrobe master, and so on. The unifying linkage of this complex process is "and then." But there is no *causal* connection. (He does not don his vestments *because* he has washed.) Such examples show that specifically *causal* processes constitute only a particular kind among the processes we encounter in nature, though, of course, its role in *natural* philosophy is paramount.

3. Stephen Pepper, *Aesthetic Quality* (New York: C. Scribners, 1938), p. 71.

4. William James, *A Pluralistic Universe*, 350.

5. Whitehead, *Process and Reality*, 21/31.

5. PROCESS PHILOSOPHY OF NATURE (PP. 83–103)

1. Whitehead was so strong an organicist that for him the principle that ontogenesis implicates phylogenesis is replicated at the cosmic level: "An actual entity cannot be a member of a 'common world', except in the sense that the 'common world' is a constituent of its own constitution. It follows that every item of the universe, including all the other actual entities, is a constituent in the constitution in any one actual entity" (*Process and Reality*, 148/224). This is orthodox Leibnizian doctrine (every monad in its composition mirrors the entire world, "from its own point of view").

This standpoint carries the idea of the connectedness of the world's processes to its ultimate—perhaps exaggerated—extreme.

2. Carl G. Hempel, "Science Unlimited," *Annals of the Japan Association for Philosophy of Science* 14 (1973): 187–202 (see 200). Italics.

3. Note, too, that the question of the existence of facts is a horse of a very different color from that of the existence of things. There being no things is undoubtedly a possible situation; there being no facts is not (since if the situation were realized, this would itself constitute a fact).

4. David Hume, *Dialogues concerning Natural Religion*, ed. N. K. Smith (London: Macmillan, 1922), 189.

5. G. W. Leibniz, "Principles of Nature and of Grace," sec. 8, italics. Cf. Saint Thomas: "Of necessity, therefore, anything in process of change is being changed by something else" (*Summa Theologica*, Ia, q. 2, art. 3). The idea that only substances can produce changes goes back to Thomas's master, Aristotle. In Plato and the pre-Socratics, the causal efficacy of principles is recognized (e.g., the love and strife of Empedocles).

6. Aristotle taught that every change must emanate from a "mover," a substance whose machinations provide the cause of change. This commitment to causal reification is at work in much of the history of Western thought. That its impetus is manifest at virtually every historical juncture is clear from William Lane Craig's interesting study, *The Cosmological Argument from Plato to Leibniz* (London: Macmillan, 1980).

7. One of the very few voices ever raised in opposition to the idea that only existing causes can have existing effects is that of Speusippus, Plato's nephew and successor as head of the Academy, who is sometimes interpreted as having taught that the world of existing things depends upon a principle, the One, that is not itself an existing thing. See R. M. Dancy, "Ancient Non-Beings: Speusippus and Others," *Ancient Philosophy* 9 (1989): 207–43.

8. On these issues see the present author's *Riddle of Existence* (Lanham, MD: University Press of America, 1984).

9. Teilhard de Chardin, *The Future of Man*, trans. Norman Dewey (New York: Harper & Row, 1969), 261.

10. Ibid., 88.

11. Ibid., 84.

12. The work of I. Prigogine in nonequilibrium thermodynamics is particularly suggestive here. It shows empirically that complex random processes in nature tend to evolve systems of organization as lowest-possible entropy states, so that self-organization is consistent with the second law of thermodynamics rather than conflicting with it. This has far-reaching implications for the evolution of "higher," more complex forms of order in nature, and reinforces process philosophy's feasible view of the systemic and organic.

13. George Herbert Mead, *The Philosophy of the Present* (La Salle, IL: Open Court, 1932), 1.

14. Ibid.

15. George Herbert Mead, "The Nature of the Past," in *Selected Writings*, ed. Andrew J. Reck (Indianapolis: Bobbs-Merrill, 1964), 349.

16. Ibid., 345.

17. John Dewey, "Time and Individuality," in *Time and Its Mysteries*, ed. Harlow Shapley (New York: Collier Books, 1962), 141–59, esp. 157.

18. On these issues compare the present author's *A Useful Inheritance* (Savage, MD: Rowman & Littlefield, 1990).

19. See *Process and Reality*, 94–95/145–46, 238–39/365–66.

20. See especially Whitehead's *Concept of Nature*; and Whitehead's *The Principle of Relativity* (Cambridge: Cambridge University Press, 1922).

21. On these issues see Edward Pols, *Whitehead's Metaphysics* (Carbondale, IL: Southern Illinois University Press, 1967).

22. See H. James Birx, *Pierre Teilhard de Chardin's Philosophy of Evolution* (Springfield, IL: Charles C. Thomas, 1972).

23. Various aspects of cultural evolutions are interestingly treated in Robert Byrd and Peter J. Richardson, *Culture and the Evolutionary Process* (Chicago: University of Chicago Press, 1985). Their deliberations indicate that cultural evolution is not just an analogue of biological evolution but that both are variant forms of one structurally uniform process.

24. This separates process philosophers from other evolution-inspired thinkers whose views are pessimistic and nonprogressivistic—for example, Nietzsche, with his doctrine of eternal recurrence.

25. On these themes see George R. Lucas Jr., "Evolutionist Theories and Whitehead's Philosophy," *Process Studies* 14 (1985): 287–300; and also the chapter "Evolution and the Emergence of Process Metaphysics" in his *Rehabilitation of Whitehead.* Lucas highlights the role in Whitehead's metaphysics of the salient ideas of evolutionary cosmology.

26. The methodology at issue is set out more fully in the present author's *Methodological Pragmatism* (Oxford: Basil Blackwell, 1972).

27. Whitehead saw the linkage between philosophy and science as so intimate as to cast cosmology in philosophy's traditional role of the queen of the sciences: "Cosmology, since it is the outcome of the highest generality of speculation, is the critic of all speculation inferior to itself in generality" (*The Function of Reason* [Boston: Beacon Press, 1929], 86).

6. PROCESS AND PERSONS (PP. 105–122)

1. David Hume, *A Treatise of Human Nature*, bk. II, pt. IV, sect. 6, "Of Personal Identity." In the appendix, Hume elaborates further: "When I turn my reflection on *myself*, I never can perceive this *self* without some one or more perceptions; nor can I ever perceive anything but the perceptions. It is the composition of these, therefore, which forms the SELF."

2. "Bad Faith" in *Being and Nothingness*, trans. Hazel Barnes (New York: Washington Square Press, 1966), 107ff.

3. Our sense of self is (as process philosophy sees it) the glimmering insight of pat of the whole to which it sees itself as belonging.

4. John Dewey, "Time and Individuality," in *Time and Its Mysteries*, ed. Harlow Shapley (New York: Collier Books, 1952), 141–59 (see 146).

5. Jean-Paul Sartre, Being and Nothingness trans Hazel E. Barnes (New York: Philosophical Library, 1948), see esp. 291.

6. See George Herbert Mead, *Philosophy of the Present*; and idem, *Mind, Self, and Society from the Standpoint of a Social Behaviorist* (Chicago: University of Chicago Press, 1934). On Mead's thought see Anselm Strass, *The Social Psychology of George Herbert Mead* (Chicago: University of Chicago Press, 1956).

7. Miguel de Unamuno, *Del sentimiento trágico de la vida*, ed. P. Felix Garcia (Madrid: Editorial Calpe 1982), p. 52.

8. Compare John B. Cobb and David R. Griffin, *Process Theology: An Introductory Exposition* (Philadelphia: Westminster Press, 1976).

9. For these problems see George R. Lucas, Jr., *The Rehabilitation of Whitehead*, 144–49.

10. Whitehead, *Adventures of Ideas*, 297–98.

11. Charles Hartshorne, "The Development of Process Philosophy," in *Process Theology: Basic Writings*, ed. Ewert H. Cousins (New York: Newman Press, 1971).

12. "Ships and agriculture, fortifications and laws, arms, road, clothing, and all else of this kind, life's prizes, and also all its luxuries, poetry and pictures, the shaping of statues by the artist, all these as men progressed gradually step by step were taught by practice and the experiements of the active mind" (*De rerum natura*, V, 1448–55).

13. The classic account is that of J. B. Bury, *The Idea of Progress* (London: Macmillan, 1932). An instructive study of more specialized scope is Ludwig Edelstein, *The Idea of Progress in Classical Antiquity* (Baltimore: Johns Hopkins University Press, 1967). See also E. R. Dodds, *The Ancient Concept of Progress and Other Essays* (Oxford: Clarendon Press, 1973).

14. *Measure for Measure*, V. 1.

15. Plato, *Symposium*, 208A–B, trans. Benjamin Jowett.

7. PROCESS LOGIC AND EPISTEMOLOGY (PP. 123–137)

1. The static *being* of the Western theory of logic and language has led various philosophers (Henri Bergson perhaps most prominent among them) to deny the adequacy of these instrumentalities vis à vis a world of activity and change. But rather than

simply deny the competency of logic and language per se, it would seem more plausible to argue the need for their extension and enhancement. And this the direction in which modern developments have, in fact, moved. Some account of these developments is given in Nicholas Rescher and Alasdair Urquhart, *Temporal Logic* (New York: Springer Verlag, 1971).

2. Whitehead seems to have something of this sort in view when he writes: "The interests of logic, dominating over intellectualized philosophers, have obscured the main functions of propositions in the nature of things. They are not primarily for belief but . . . constitute a source for the origination of feeling which is not tied down to a mere dictum" (*Process and Reality*, 186/283). On these issues see also George R. Lucas Jr., *The Rehabilitation of Whitehead*, 141–44.

3. Aristotle's sea-battle discussion has been widely—and diversely—analyzed in recent years. For the older literature, see Nicholas Rescher, "Aristotle's Doctrine of Future Contingency and Excluded Middle," in *Studies in the History of Arab Logic* (Pittsburgh: University of Pittsburgh Press, 1963), 43–54; and J. L. Ackrill, *Aristotle's Categories and "De Interpretatione,"* tr. with notes (Oxford: Clarendon Press, 1963), esp. 132–42; Christopher Kirwan, *Aristotle's Metaphysics, Books Gamma, Delta, and Epsilon,* tr. with notes (Oxford: Clarendon Press, 1971), esp. 189–98. More recent treatments include Richard Sorabji, *Necessity, Cause, and Blame* (Ithaca, NY: Cornell University Press, 1980), chap. 5; Sarah Waterlow, *Passage and Possibility* (Oxford: Clarendon Press, 1982), chap. 5; L. D. Harris, "Solving the Naval Battle," *Aristotelian Society Proceedings*, vol. 77 (1977/8); M. J. White, "Fatalism and Causal Determination," *Philosophical Quarterly* (1981); Dorothea Frede, "The Sea Battle Reconsidered: A Defence of the Traditional Interpretation," *Oxford Studies in Ancient Philosophy*, ed. by Julia Annas (Oxford: Clarendon Press), Vol. 3 (1985), 31–88.

4. *On Generation and Corruption.* II, ii and *Metaphysics.* VI, 2–3 are also relevant here. See also C. J. F. Williams, *Aristotle's "De Generatione et Corruptione,"* tr. with notes (Oxford: Clarendon Press, 1982), esp. 197–210.

5. The themes of this section are developed from other points of departure in present author's *The Limits of Science* (Berkeley: University of California Press, 1985).

6. These stages mirror closely C. S. Peirce's triadic conception of the meaning relation in terms of referent sign-or-symbol/interpretant. For Peirce's theory of meaning, see Murray G. Murphy, *The Development of Peirce's Philosophy* (Cambridge MA: Harvard University Press, 1961).

7. For a good development of this approach to the process theory of symbol use in relation to knowledge and information, see Harold N. Lee, "Process and Pragmatism," in *Studies in Process Philosophy*, ed. Robert C. Littlemore (New Orleans: Tulane University Press, 1974) 87º97.

8. See George Lakoff and Mark Johnson, *Metaphors We Live By* (Chicago: University of Chicago Press, 1982).

8. A PROCESSUAL VIEW OF SCIENTIFIC INQUIRY (PP. 139–151)

1. *Veniet tempus quo posteri nostri tam aperta nos nescisse mirentur.* "There will come a time when our descendants will be amazed that we did not know things that are so plain to them" (Seneca, *Natural Questions*, VII, 25,,5).

2. See Charles Perrow, *Normal Accidents* (New York: Basic Books, 1989).

3. For a further account of the relevant considerations see *The Limits of Science.*

4. Frederick Soddy, *Science and Life* (New York: E. P. Dutton, 1930).

5. Quoted by Gerald Holton, "Scientific Progress," *Daedalus* 107 (1978), 24.

6. Baden Powell, *Essays on the Spirit of the Inductive Philosophy* (London: Longman, 1855), 23.

7. The role of unforeseeable innnovations in science forms a key part of Popper's case against the unpredictability of man's social affairs—given that new science engenders new technologies which in turn make for new modes of social organization. (See K. R. Popper, *The Poverty of Historicism* [London: Routledge & Kegan paul, 1957], vi and passim). A balanced treatment of the issues is given in Alex Rosenberg, "Scientific Innovation and the Limits of Social Scientific Prediction," *Synthese* 97 (1993): 161–81. On the

present issue Rosenberg cites the anecdote of the musician who answered the question "Where is jazz heading?" with the response, "If I knew that, I'd be there already" (ibid., 167). On this issue see also Lutz Dannenberg, *Methodologien: Struktur, Aufbau and Evaluation* (Berlin: Duncker & Humblot, 1989).

8. And this holds for technology as well through the principle of "equivalent invention," described by S. C. Gilfillan in 1939. (For the references see S. Colum Gilfillan, "A Sociologist Looks at Technical Prediction," in *Technical Forecasting for Industry and Government*, ed. James R. Wright [Englewood Cliffs, NJ: Prentice Hall; 1968]). Instancing the problem of flying aircraft in fog, Gilfillan notes that some dozen different ways of addressing it were under consideration in the 1930s. But which method would prove most successful and thus prevail was imponderable. That the problem would be resolved could be predicted with confidence but *how* was unforeseeable.

9. D. A. Bromley et al., *Physics in Perspective* (Washington, DC: National Academy of Science, 1973), 16, 23. See also Gerald Holton, "Models for Understanding the Growth and Excellence of Scientific Research," in *Excellence and Leadership in a Democracy*, ed. Stephen R. Graubard and Gerald Holton (New York: Random House, 1962), 115.

10. A fishing analogy of Eddington's is useful here. He saw the experimentalists as akin to a fisherman who trawls nature with the net of his equipment for detection and observation. Now suppose (says Eddington) that a fisherman trawls the seas using a fishnet of two-inch mesh. Then fish of a smaller size will simply go uncaught, and those who analyze the catch will have an incomplete and distorted view of aquatic life. The situation in science is the same. Only by improving our observational means of trawling nature can such imperfections be mitigated. (See A. S. Eddington, *The Nature of the Physical World* [London: Macmillan, 1929]).

11. For an interesting and suggestive analysis of "the architecture of complexity," see Herbert A. Simon, *The Sciences of the Artificial* (Cambridge MA: MIT Press, 1969).

12. Some of the ideas of the final sections are developed more fully in the present author's *Scientific Progress* (Oxford: Blackwell, 1978). The book is also available in translation: German transl., *Wissenschaftlicher Fortschitt* (Berlin: De Gruyter, 1982); French transl., *Le Progrès scientifique* (Paris: Presses Universitaires de France, 1994).

9. PROCESS THEOLOGY (PP. 153–163)

1. The major process theologians include Pierre Teilhard de Chardin (1881–1955) in France; Samuel Alexander (1859–1944), Conroy Loyd Morgan (1852–1936), William Temple (1882–1944), and Lionel Spencer Thornton (1884–1947) in Britain; and Alfred North Whitehead (1861–1967) and Charles Hartshorne (1897–   ) in the United States, together with their students and followers. For fuller information about process theology, which has been an increasingly active enterprise in recent years, the reader may consult Charles Birch, *A Purpose for Everything: Religion in a Postmodern Worldview* (Mystic, CT: Twenty-Third Publications, 1990); John B. Cobb and David R. Griffin, *Process Theology*; John B. Cobb, *Process Theology as Political Ecology* (Philadelphia: Westminster Press, 1982); Charles Hartshorne, *The Divine Relativity: A Social Conception of God* (New Haven: Yale University Press, 1948); idem, *A Natural Theology for Our Time* (La Salle, IL: Open Court, 1967); A. N. Whitehead, *Religion in the Making* (Cambridge: Cambridge University Press, 1930).

For useful anthologies on the topic, see Delwin Brown et al. (eds.), *Process Philosophy and Christian Thought* (Indianapolis: Bobbs-Merrill, 1971); Douglas Browning, *Philosophers of Process* (New York: Random House, 1965); Ewert H. Cousins (ed.), *Process Theology: Basic Writings*, which seeks to fuse the organismic tradition of Whitehead with the evolutionism of Teilhard de Chardin. Also, James R. Gray's *Modern Process Thought* (Lanham, MD: University Press of America, 1982) is an anthology focused largely on process theology.

2. Interesting deliberations by Donald W. Sherburne suggest for Whitehead himself the (declined) option of a naturalistic processism. See Sherburne, "Whitehead without God," *Christian Scholar* 60 (1907): 251–72.

3. See, for example, Michael J. Buckley, *Motion and Motion's God* (Princeton: Princeton University Press, 1971).

4. On this aspect of process theology see Josiah Royce, *The World and the Individual*, 2 vols. (New York: MacMillin, 1901–1902), Vol. I, chapter entitled "The Temporal and External"; E. S. Brightman, "A Temporalist View of God," in *The Journal of Religion*, vol. 2 (1932); A. O. Lovejoy, "The Obsolescence of the Eternal," in *The Philosophical Review*, vol. 18 (1909), pp. 479–502; and J. A.

Leighton, "Time and the Logic of Monistic Idealism," in *Essays in Honor of J. E. Creighton* (New York: Macmillan, 1917), 151–161.

5. Compare Charles Valentine, "The Development of Process Philosophy," in *Process Theology: Basic Writings*, ed. Ewert H. Cousins.

6. Cf. *Process and Reality*, 374. See the report by A. H. Johnson in L. S. Ford and G. L. Kline (eds.), *Explorations in Whitehead's Philosophy* (New York: Fordham University Press, 1983), 4–10.

10. Process in Philosophy (pp. 165–174)

1. Andrew J. Reck, "Process Philosophy: A Categorical Analysis," in *Studies in Process Philosophy II*, ed. R. C. Whittemore (New Orleans: Tulane University Press, 1975), 58–91 (see 59).

2. Whitehead, *Process and Reality*, 14/21. Metaphysical claims are no more than "tentative formulations of ultimate generalities" (ibid., 8/12).

3. P. F. Strawson, *Individuals: An Essay in Descriptive Metaphysics* (London: Methuen & Co., 1959). Strawson's argumentation has been considered on pp. 60–64 above.

4. "In no other philosophy, I believe, have so many theoretical and spiritual values been united with so much appearance of consistency and clarity" (Charles Hartshorne, Introduction to *Philosophers of Process*, ed. Douglas Browning (New York: Random House, 1965).

Appendix: Process Semantics (pp. 175–182)

1. On the history of the issue see Rescher, "The Concept of Nonexistent Possibles," in *Essays in Philosophical Analysis* (Pittsburgh: University of Pittsburgh Press, 1969), 73–109.

2. W. V. Quine, "On What There Is," *Review of Metaphysics* 2 (1948): 21–38.

3. W. V. Quine, *Word and Object* (Cambridge: Harvard University Press, 1980), 179, sect. 37.

4. Quine, "On What There Is," 8.

5. Quine, *Word and Object*, 192, sect. 40, fn. 1.

6. On the logic of position see the present author's "Topological Logic," in *Topics in Philosophical Logic* (Dordrecht: D. Reidel, 1968), 229–49. The fact that the positions at issue are spatiotemporal brings temporal logic (often called "tense logic") upon the scene. For details see N. Rescher and A. Urquhart, *Temporal Logic*. Of course, given the centrality of time in process philosophy, this need to bring time upon the scene is exactly what a process philosopher would expect.

7. There is, alas, an ambiguity at work here. As Arthur Schopenhauer pointed out, there are those who live *for* philosophy and those who live *on* it. A philosopher can be a person who holds a post in philosophy at an academic institution or a person who engages in the activity of philosophizing. It is the latter sense of "philosophy" that is presently at issue. Then, too, there is the complication that to be a philosopher (in this sense) one must philosophize not just sometimes but often. But this complication can be put aside for present purposes; it can be accommodated by well-known devices. The point that *is* important for present purposes, however, is that the move from "sometimes" to "often" (or "regularly") also requires the resources of a temporal logic.

8. "The Logical Form of Action Sentences," in *The Logic of Decision and Action*, ed. Nicholas Rescher (Pittsburgh: University of Pittsburgh Press, 1967), 81.

Bibliography

Bergson, Henri. *Creative Evolution*. Trans. Arthur Mitchell. London: Macmillan, 1911.

————. *The Creative Mind*. New York: Philosophical Library, 1946.

Birch, Charles. *A Purpose for Everything: Religion in a Postmodern Worldview*. Mystic, CT: Twenty-Third Publications, 1990.

Birx, H. James. *Pierre Teilhard de Chardin's Philosophy of Evolution*. Springfield, IL: Charles C. Thomas, 1972.

Blyth, John W. *Whitehead's Theory of Knowledge*. Providence, RI: Brown University Press, 1941.

Böhme, G. "Whiteheads Abkehr von der Substanzmetaphysik" in *Whitehead: Einführung in seine Kosmologie*, ed. E. Wolf-Gazo. Munich: Verlag Karl Alber, 1980.

Brightman, E. S. "A Temporalist View of God." *Journal of Religion* 2 (1932): 102–43.

Broad, C. D. *Scientific Thought*. London: K. Paul, Trench, Treubner, 1923.

Brown, Delwin, et al. (eds.). *Process Philosophy and Christian Thought*. Indianapolis: Bobbs-Merrill, 1971.

Browning, Douglas. *Philosophers of Process*. New York: Random House, 1965.

————. "Sameness through Change and the Coincidence of Properties." *Philosophy and Phenomenological Research*, 49 (1988): 103–76.

Brumbaugh, Robert S. *Whitehead, Process Philosophy, and Education*. Albany, NY: SUNY Press, 1982.

Buchler, Justus. *The Metaphysics of Natural Complexes*. New York: Columbia University Press, 1966.

Buckley, Michael J. *Motion and Motion's God*. Princeton: Princeton University Press, 1971.

Christensen, F. M. "The Source of the River of Time." *Ratio* 18 (1976): 131–43.

Christian, William A. *An Interpretation of Whitehead's Metaphysics.* New Haven: Yale University Press, 1959.

———. "An Appraisal to Whiteheadean Nontheism." *Southern Journal of Philosophy* 15 (1967): 27–35.

Cobb, John B. *A Christian Natural Theology.* Philadelphia: Westminster Press, 1965.

———. "The Whitehead without God Dispute." *Process Studies* 1 (1971): 236–48.

Cobb, John B., and David R. Griffin. *Process Theology: An Introductory Exposition.* Philadelphia: Westminster Press, 1976.

———. *Process Theology as Political Ecology.* Philadelphia: Westminster Press, 1982.

Cousins, Ewert H. (ed.). *Process Theology: Basic Writings.* New York: Newman Press, 1971.

Dewey, John. *Experience and Nature.* Chicago: Open Court, 1925. Reprint, vol. 1 in *John Dewey, The Later Works, 1925–1953.* Carbondale, IL: Southern Illinois University Press, 1988.

———. *Logic: The Theory of Inquiry.* New York: Holt, 1938. Reprint, vol. 12 in *John Dewey, The Later Works, 1925–1953.* Carbondale, IL: Southern Illinois University Press, 1986.

Emmet, Dorothy. *Whitehead's Philosophy of Organism.* 2d ed. New York: St. Martin's Press, 1966.

Fetz, R. L. *Whitehead: Processdenken und Substanzmetaphysik.* Munich: Verlag Karl Alber, 1981.

Ford, Lewis S. *The Emergence of Whitehead's Metaphysics, 1925–1929.* Albany, NY: SUNY Press, 1984.

Ford, Lewis S. (ed.). *Two Process Philosophers: Hartshorne's Encounter with Whitehead.* Tallahassee, FL: American Academy of Religion, 1973.

Ford, Lewis S., and George L. Kline (eds.). *Explorations in Whitehead's Philosophy.* New York: Fordham University Press, 1983.

Frede, Dorothea. "The Sea Battle Reconsidered: A Defence of the Traditional Interpretation." *Oxford Studies in Ancient Philosophy* 3 (1985): 128–42.

Geiger, George R. *John Dewey in Perspective.* Oxford: Oxford University Press, 1958.

Gray, James R. *Modern Process Thought.* Lanham, MD: University of America, 1982.

Grünbaum, Adolf. "Whitehead's Method of Extensive Abstraction." *British Journal for the Philosophy of Science* 4 (1953): 215–226.

———. "A. N. Whitehead's Philosophy of Science." *Philosophical Review* 71 (1962): 218–229.

———. *Modern Science and Zeno's Paradoxes.* London: Allen & Unwin, 1967.

Gunter, P. A. Y. *Bergson and the Evolution of Physics.* Knoxville, TN: University of Tennessee Press, 1969.

Hacker, P. M. S. "Events and Objects in Space and Time." *Mind* 91 (1982): 1–19.

Hahn, Lewis (ed.). *The Philosophy of Charles Hartshorne.* La Salle, IL: Open Court, 1991.

Hammerschmidt, W. W. *Whitehead's Philosophy of Time.* New York: Russell & Russell, 1975.

Hartshorne, Charles. "Contingency and the New Era in Metaphysics." *Journal of Philosophy* 29 (1932): 421–431, 457–469.

———. *Creative Synthesis and Philosophic Method.* La Salle, IL: Open Court, 1970.

———. "The Development of Process Philosophy." In *Process Theology*, ed. Ewert H. Cousins. New York: Newman Press, 1971.

———. *The Divine Relativity: A Social Conception of God.* New Haven: Yale University Press, 1948.

———. *A Natural Theology for Our Time.* La Salle, IL: Open Court, 1967.

———. *Whitehead's Philosophy: Selected Essays, 1935–1970.* Lincoln, NB: University of Nebraska Press, 1972.

Hawks, Donald. "Process as a Categorical Concept." In *Studies in Process Philosophy, II*, ed. R. C. Whittemore. New Orleans: Tulane University Press, 1975.

Holz, Harald, and Ernst Wolf-Gazo (eds.). *Whitehead und der Prozessbegriff*. Munich: Verlag Karl Alber, 1984.

James, William. *The Principles of Psychology*. 2 vols. New York: Henry Holt & Co., 1890.

———. *A Pluralistic Universe*. New York: Longmans, Green, 1910.

———. *Some Problems of Philosophy*. New York: Longmans, Green, 1911.

———. *The Writings of William James*. Ed. John J. MacDermott. Chicago: University of Chicago Press, 1977.

Johnson, A. H. *Whitehead's Theory of Reality*. New York: Dover Publications, 1952.

Kane, Robert, and Stephen H. Phillips (eds.). *Hartshorne, Process Philosophy, and Theology*. Albany, NY: SUNY Press, 1989.

Kline, George L. (ed.). *Alfred North Whitehead: Essays on His Philosophy*. Englewood Cliffs, NJ: Prentice Hall, 1963.

Kneale, William. "The Notion of a Substance." *Proceedings of the Aristotelian Society* 39 (1939/40): 103–39.

Kolakowski, Lesek. *Bergson*. New York: Oxford University Press, 1985.

Kraus, Elizabeth M. *The Metaphysics of Experience: A Companion to Whitehead's "Process and Reality."* New York: Fordham University Press, 1979.

Lango, John W. *Whitehead's Ontology*. Albany, NY: SUNY Press, 1972.

Lawrence, Nathaniel. *Whitehead's Philosophical Development*. Berkeley: University of California Press, 1956.

Leclerc, Ivor. *Whitehead's Metaphysics: An Introductory Exposition*. Bloomington, IL: Indiana University Press, 1958.

———. *The Relevance of Whitehead*. London: Allen & Unwin, 1961.

Lee, Harold N. "Process and Pragmatism." In *Studies in Process Philosophy*, ed. Robert C. Littlemore, 87–97. New Orleans: Tulane University Press, 1974.

Leue, W. "Process and Essence." *Philosophy and Phenomenological Research* 21 (1960): 62–78.

Levinson, A. B. "Events and Time's Flow." *Mind* 96 (1987): 341–53.

Lombard, L. B. *Events: A Metaphysical Study.* London: Routledge & Kegan Paul, 1986.

Lovejoy, A. O. "The Obsolescence of the Eternal." *Philosophical Review* 18 (1909): 479–502.

Lowe, Victor. *Understanding Whitehead.* Baltimore: Johns Hopkins University Press, 1962.

———. *Alfred North Whitehead: The Man and His Work, 1861–1900.* Baltimore: Johns Hopkins University Press, 1985.

Lucas, George R. Jr. *Two Views of Freedom in Process Thought: A Study of Hegel and Whitehead.* Missoula, MN: Scholar's Press, 1979.

———. *The Genesis of Modern Process Thought.* Metuchen, NJ: Scarecrow Press, 1983.

———. *Hegel and Whitehead: Contemporary Perspectives on Systematic Philosophy.* Albany: SUNY Press, 1986.

———. *The Rehabilitation of Whitehead: An Analytical and Historical Arsenal of Process Philosophy.* Albany, NY: SUNY Press, 1989.

Macdonald, Margaret. "Things and Processes." *Analysis* 6 (1938): 1–10.

McTaggart, J. M. E. *The Nature of Existence.* 2 vols. Cambridge: Cambridge University Press, 1921.

Mays, Wolf. *The Philosophy of Whitehead.* London: Allen & Unwin, 1959.

———. *Whitehead's Philosophy of Science and Metaphysics.* The Hague: Martinus Nijhoff, 1977.

Mead, George Herbert. *The Philosophy of the Present.* La Salle, IL: Open Court, 1932.

———. *Selected Writings.* Ed. Andrew J. Reck. Indianapolis: Bobbs-Merrill, 1964.

Miller, David L., and George V. Gentry. *The Philosophy of A. N. Whitehead.* Minneapolis: Burgess, 1938.

Morgan, C. Lloyd. *Emergent Evolution.* New York: Henry Holt, 1925.

Mouralatos, A. "Events, Processes, and States." *Linguistics and Philosophy* 2 (1978): 415–34.

Nash, Ronald H. (ed.). *Process Theology.* Grand Rapids, MI: Baker Book House, 1987.

Neville, Robert C. *Creativity and God: A Challenge to Process Theology.* New York: Seabury Press, 1980.

Nobo, Jorge Luis. *Whitehead's Metaphysics of Extension and Solidarity.* Albany, NY: SUNY Press, 1986.

Palter, Robert M. *Whitehead's Philosophy of Science.* Chicago: University of Chicago Press, 1960.

Pittinger, Norman. *Alfred North Whitehead.* Richmond, VA: John Knox Press, 1969.

Plamondon, Ann L. *Whitehead's Organic Philosophy of Science.* Albany, NY: SUNY Press, 1979.

Pols, Edward R. *Whitehead's Metaphysics: A Critical Examination of Process and Reality.* Carbondale, IL: Southern Illinois University Press, 1967.

Prigogine, Ilya. *From Being to Becoming.* New York: Freeman & Co., 1980.

Quine, W. V. *Word and Object.* Cambridge, MA: Harvard University Press 1980.

———. "On What There Is." *Review of Metaphysics* 2 (1948): 21–38;. Reprinted in *From a Logical Point of View.* Cambridge, MA: Harvard University Press, 1953.

Quinton, A. N. "Objects and Events." *Mind* 88 (1970): 197–214.

Reck, Andrew J. "Process Philosophy: A Categorical Analysis." In *Studies in Process Philosophy, II* ed. R. C. Whittemore, 58–91. New Orleans: Tulane University, 1975.

Reese, William L., and Eugene Freeman (eds.). *Process and Divinity: The Hartshorne Festschrift.* La Salle, IL: Open Court, 1964.

Rescher, Nicholas. "The Revolt against Process." *Journal of Philosophy* 59 (1962): 410–17.

————. "Aristotle's Doctrine of Future Contingency and Excluded Middle." In *Studies in the History of Arabic Logic*, 43–54. Pittsburgh: University of Pittsburgh Press, 1963.

————. "Aspects of Action." In *The Logic of Decision and Action*, ed. Nicholas Rescher, 215–19. Pittsburgh: University of Pittsburgh Press, 1967.

————. *Conceptual Idealism.* Oxford: Basil Blackwell, 1973.

Rescher, Nicholas, and Alexander Urquhart. *Temporal Logic.* New York: Springer Verlag, 1971.

Roberts, J. H. "Actions and Performances Considered as Objects and Events." *Philosophical Studies* 35 (1979): 171–85.

Ross, Stephen David. *Perspectives in Whitehead's Metaphysics.* Albany, NY: SUNY Press, 1983.

Royce, Josiah. *The World and the Individual.* 2 vols. New York: Macmillan, 1901–1902.

Schiller, F. C. S. "Metaphysics of the Time-Process." *Mind* 4 (1895): 36–46.

————. "Novelty." In *Proceedings of the Aristotelian Society* 22 (1922–1923): 1–22.

————. *The Philosophy of John Dewey.* Evanston, IL: Northwestern University Press, 1939.

Schilpp, Paul Arthur (ed.). *The Philosophy of Alfred North White-head.* Evanston, IL: Northwestern University Press, 1941; expanded edition, 1951.

Schmidt, Paul F. *Perception and Cosmolgy in Whitehead's Philosophy.* New Brunswick, NJ: Rutgers University Press, 1967.

Seibt, Johanna. "Towards Process Ontology: A Critical Study in Substance-Ontological Premises. PhD. diss., University of Pittsburgh, 1990.

————. *Properties as Processes: A Synoptic Study of W. Sellars' Nominalism.* Reseda, CA: Ridgeview, 1990.

Sellars, Wilfrid. "Foundations of a Metaphysics of Pure Process." *Monist* 64 (1987): 3–90.

Shahan, E. P. *Whitehead's Theory of Experience.* New York: King's Crown Press, 1950.

Sherburne, Donald W. *A Key to Whitehead's Process and Reality*. New York: Macmillan, 1966; Chicago: University of Chicago Press, 1986.

———. *A Whiteheadian Aesthetic*. New Haven: Yale University Press, 1967.

———. "Whitehead without God." *Christian Scholar* 40 (1967): 251–72.

Sibley, Jack R., and Peter A. Y. Gunter. *Process Philosophy: Basic Writings*. Lanham, MD: University Press of America, 1978.

Singer, Beth. "Substitutes for Substances." *Modern Schoolman* 53 (1975): 19–38.

Smart, J. J. C. "The River of Time." In *Essays in Conceptual Analysis*, A.G.N. Flew (ed.), 263–67. London: Methuen, 1966.

Sorabji, Richard. *Necessity, Cause, and Blame*. Ithaca, NY: Cornell University Press, 1980.

Stokes, Walter E. "A Selected and Annotated Bibliography of A. N. Whitehead." *Modern Schoolman* 39 (1962): 135–53.

Strawson, P. F. *Individuals: An Essay in Descriptive Metaphysics*. 4th ed. London: Methuen, 1987.

Sweet, Dennis. *Heraclitus: Translation and Analysis*. Lanham, MD: University Press of America, 1995.

Teilhard de Chardin, Pierre. *The Future of Man*. Trans. Norman Dewey. New York: Harper & Row, 1964.

Thompson, Kenneth F. Jr. *Whitehead's Philosophy of Religion*. The Hague: Mouton, 1971.

Unamuno, Miguel de. *Del sentimiento trágico de la vida*. Ed. P. Felix Garcia. Madrid, Espasa-Calpe, 1982.

Ushenko, Andrew Paul. *Power and Events*. Princeton: Princeton University Press, 1946; Chicago: University of Chicago Press, 1986.

Valentine, Charles. "The Development of Process Philosophy." In *Process Theology: Basic Writings*, ed. Ewert H. Cousins. New York, Newman Press, 1971.

Wallack, F. Bradford. *The Epochal Nature of Process in Whitehead's Metaphysics*. Albany, NY: SUNY Press, 1980.

Waterlow, Sarah. *Passage and Possibility*. Oxford: Oxford University Press, 1982.

Weiss, Paul. *Reality*. Princeton, NJ: Princeton University Press, 1938.

Wells, Harry K. *Process and Unreality*. New York: King's Crown Press, 1950.

White, M. J. "Fatalism and Causal Determinism." *Philosophical Quarterly* 31 (1981): 231–41.

Whitehead, A. N. *An Enquiry Concerning the Principles of Natural Knowledge*. Cambridge: Cambridge University Press, 1919; New York: Kraus Reprints, 1982.

———. *The Concept of Nature*. Cambridge: Cambridge University Press, 1920.

———. *The Principle of Relativity*. Cambridge: Cambridge University Press, 1922.

———. *Science and the Modern World*. New York: Macmillan, 1925.

———. *Religion in the Making*. New York: Macmillan, 1926.

———. *Process and Reality: An Essay in Cosmology*. New York: Macmillan, 1929. Critical edition by D. R. Griffin and D.W. Sherbourne. New York: Macmillan, 1978.

———. *Symbolism: Its Meaning and Effect*. New York: Macmillan, 1927; New York: G. P. Putnam's Sons, 1959.

———. *The Function of Reason*. Boston: Beacon Press, 1929.

———. *Adventures of Ideas*. New York: Macmillan, 1933.

———. *Nature and Life*. Cambridge: Cambridge University Press, 1934.

———. *Modes of Thought*. New York: Macmillan, 1938.

———. *Essays in Science and Philosophy*. New York: Philosophical Library, 1948.

Whittemore, Robert C. (ed.). *Studies in Process Philosophy*. New Orleans: Tulane University Press, 1974.

———. *Studies in Process Philosophy, II.* New Orleans: Tulane University Press, 1976.

———. *Studies in Process Philosophy, III.* New Orleans: Tulane University Press, 1975.

Whorf, R. F. *Language, Thought, and Reality.* Ed. J. Carroll. Cambridge: MIT Press, 1956.

Wiggins, David. *Identity and Spatio-Temporal Continuity.* Oxford: Basil Blackwell, 1967.

Wild, John. *The Radical Empiricism of William James.* Garden City, NY: Doubleday, 1969.

———. *Sameness and Substance.* Cambridge: Harvard University Press, 1980.

Wolf-Gazo, Ernst. *Whitehead: Einführung in seine Kosmologie.* Munich: Verlag Karl Alber, 1980.

Zemach, Edward. "Four Ontologies." *Journal of Philosophy* 63 (1970): 231–47.

Name Index

Alexander, Samuel, 197n1
Aquinas, St., Thomas, 158, 190n5
Aristotle, 4, 7, 10-12, 29, 36, 37, 43, 52, 67, 106, 123, 124, 126-29, 154, 167, 184n5, 187n1, 190n5, 190n6, 193n3

Ballamy, Edward, 119
Bergson, Henri, 3, 7, 15-21, 24, 35, 37, 38, 30, 77, 80, 96, 121, 185n19, 185n20, 185n21, 193n1
Berkeley, George, 52, 125
Birch, Charles, 197n1
Birx, H., James, 191n22
Boscovitch, R. J., 8, 39, 55
Bradley, F. H., 131
Brightman, E. S., 197n4
Browning, Douglas, 197n1
Buckley, Michael, J., 197n3
Bunge, Mario, 33, 187n2
Bury, J. B., 193n13
Byrd, Robert, 191n23

Calvin, John, 159
Carr, H. W., 185n21
Chardin, Peirre Teilhard de, 90, 100, 190n9, 197n1
Christian, William, Jr., 183n1
Cobb, John, B., Jr., 26, 193n8, 197n1
Comte, Auguste, 119
Craig, William, Lane, 190n6

Dancy, R. M., 190n7
Dannenberg, Lutz, 196n7
Darwin, Charles, 81
Deledalle, Gérard, 26, 187n42
Democritus, 8
Descartes, René, 52, 59, 110, 111, 125
Dewey, John, 4, 7, 14, 18-20, 25, 35, 97, 108, 124, 185n23, 185n26, 191n17, 192n4
Davidson, Donald, 179
Dodds, E. R., 193n13

Eddington, Arthur, 196n10
Edelstein, Ludwig, 193n13
Einstein, Albert, 20
Epicurus, 8, 81

Findlay, J. N., 184n7
Flower, Elizabeth, 185n18
Fontenelle, Bernard, de, 119
Ford, Lewis, S., 26
Frede, Dorothea, 194n3

Geiger, George, R., 185n26
Gilfillin, S. C., 196n8
Goudge, Thomas, A., 184n10
Gray, James, R., 197n1
Griffin, David, R., 193n8, 197n1

Harris, L. D., 194n3
Hartshorne, Charles, 25, 35, 59, 60, 113, 156, 193n11, 197n1, 198n4